Life Lens

LIFE LENS

SEEING YOUR CHILDREN IN COLOR

MICHELE MONAHAN HORNER

MCP Books | *Minneapolis*

MCP Books
322 1st Ave North, 5th Floor
Minneapolis, MN 55401
612.455.2293
www.mcpbooks.com

ISBN-13: 978-1-63505-060-8
LCCN: 2016906447

Distributed by Itasca Books

Cover Design by C. Tramell
Typeset by M.K. Ross
Edited by Amy Plattsmier

Printed in the United States of America

For my mom, Rosalie,

and my daughter, Mercedes,

with much love.

CONTENTS

Preface: Who Am I? Who Are You? ix

Introduction: People Are Similar and Different xiii

Chapter 1: Seeing the Light—Nine Windows 1

Chapter 2: The Colors of *Life Lens* 21
      Red 21
      Orange 21
      Yellow 22
      Green 22
      Blue 22
      Indigo 23
      Violet. 24

Chapter 3: Art Imitating Life 69

Chapter 4: Strategies for Success: DO's and DON'TS 87

Chapter 5: Despite *Life Lens*—Environment,
      Procrastination, and Praise 115

Chapter 6: Life Lens Diagnostic Tools 119

Appendix: The IKEA Tool 141

Appendix: Life Lens Practice Do's and Don'ts 145

References 155

Acknowledgments 159

About the Author 163

When teaching children, an adult should "come down to their physical limitations and up to their sense of wonder and awe."

- Dr. Shinichi Suzuki (1983)

PREFACE: WHO AM I?

It's a typical day. I walk into a room filled with three- to four-year-old boys and hold them in rapt attention for an hour. During this time they follow my directions. They do not wander around the room. They do not speak without raising their hands. They do not interrupt the proceedings.

When I stand up, they stand up. When I sit down, they sit down. Are they little robots? Decidedly no. Each boy has his own unique persona, but when we are together we work together toward our common objective of playing classical guitar in ensemble. "CLASSICAL GUITAR?!" you ask. Are they special kids? Maybe super talented or something? Of course they are special . . . all kids are special! But other than that, no, they are not in the preschool chapter of Mensa. They are typical little kids who do typical little kid things: they run around, they play with everything, they are curious, some like to climb things, some like to crawl under things, they talk about whatever comes to mind. These kids could be any kids; they could be your kids.

The parents of my beginner guitar group marvel at my ability to get their kids to all focus and play the guitar with good posture, beautiful tone, and excellent technique without ever raising my voice or issuing a threat. Am I the pied piper? No. I am a seasoned Suzuki method music teacher and an expert on motivating people. While my specific area of expertise lies in teaching classical guitar to children from toddlers to teenagers, over my seventeen years of professional experience, I've discovered, decoded, and researched some simple, universal principles about human learning that are completely applicable and transferable to whatever activity a child is doing.

My entire teaching approach is informed by first knowing what type of person my student is and then reaching out to him in a way that makes what I have to say easy for him to understand and take in. Through simple recognition of what motivates and what demotivates a particular student, I can predict how she will learn best and tailor my teaching strategies accordingly. My approach is a system that lays out how all people, young and old, see their living and working lives through different colored lenses and why recognizing both our own and others' colors will make learning and teaching easier. I call this system *Life Lens*.

As a Suzuki method music teacher, I am in a uniquely fortunate position because I get to spend two classes a week with children and their parents together over many years. A typical Suzuki student will start studying her instrument at age three or four and may keep at it through her teens, the parent alongside her in classes all the while. As a result I have been lucky to spend the past decade and a half studying, decoding, and using the universal learning principles I call *Life Lens* with students and their parents over a long period of time in my guitar studio, in group clinics worldwide, in conservatory settings, in classrooms, in both long-term and short-term student relationships, and with other teachers and their programs.

Life Lens is why I am a renowned leader in my field and a sought-after clinician who has trained and worked with teachers and students at music institutes and workshops all over the world. *Life Lens* is what I use to almost instantly identify students, allowing me to take advantage of their learning and thinking styles and to motivate them in the best way for them to receive the instruction I am offering. In my travels I have taught hundreds of kids and their parents in clinics where I get only a fifteen-minute lesson window with a family I have never met before. By applying the principles of *Life Lens*, I can immediately hone in, figure out what makes the student tick, and make the most of our short learning time together. It appears dramatic to those who observe, but I assure you it is not magic, just *Life Lens!*

I am excited to share the universal principles of *Life Lens* with you. As you apply them, you will see a hugely positive effect on your teaching, your parenting, and on your relationships with your children, your spouse, and your colleagues. You will never see the world in black and white again.

WHO ARE YOU?

Now that you know a little about me and why I wrote this book, I'd like to know who you are. Only kidding . . . I *already* know who you are! You're a person who is interested in understanding best practices for communicating with those around you. You'd like to foster efficient learning and better teamwork and avoid unnecessary relationship collisions. I assure you that even though I've written from my vantage point as a Suzuki guitar teacher, the principles I discuss are universal and have manifold applications in any area of teaching and learning.

You will benefit from reading this book if you are a:
- parent
- educator
- administrator
- social worker
- guidance counselor

- human resources professional
- coach
- business owner
- Suzuki music teacher
- person who interacts with other human beings

More specifically, which *Life Lens* type are you? As you continue to read, you will probably see yourself in one of chapter two's seven sections describing the behaviors of each *Life Lens* type (red, orange, yellow, green, blue, indigo, or violet). For some people, their "Aha!" moment occurs when they see the examples in chapter three of different *Life Lens* types in famous fictional or nonfictional characters and realize that the reason they've always loved *that* particular character is because they share the same *Life Lens*. Other people find it easier to discern their *Life Lens* type by first identifying their best learning style and then working backward from there.

If after reading the character and color descriptions you are still unsure about your *Life Lens* type, you can refer to the diagnostics in chapter six and try some of my fun diagnostic activities. They are quick, organic, and easy, but, while the diagnostics can be helpful, there is nothing better than the simple power of observation to help you find your color. I repeat, the *number one* method for determining a person's *Life Lens* life lens type is *observing behavior*, both in yourself and in others. Like anything in life, it only takes practice!

INTRODUCTION to *Life Lens*— PEOPLE ARE SIMILAR AND DIFFERENT

As any experienced teacher will observe, not all children learn the same. Through the years, I've often noticed in my lessons how one teaching technique would work marvelously well with one student but would fail miserably with the next. Based on these observations I made the obvious conclusion: **People are different**.

My childhood literary hero, Agatha Christie, created a character named Jane Marple. Miss Marple lived a sheltered life in a small village, yet she solved complex crimes in large unfamiliar locations based almost solely on her knowledge of the people in her village. When faced with a new circumstance, Miss Marple always compared the new situation to something or someone she knew from her past. Her investigative approach centered around the conclusion: **People are similar.**

Pondering these truths—people are both similar and different—fueled my quest to discover a simple, organic, and effective approach to identifying what makes people learn in different ways and how we can find commonality as teachers and students. I wanted to learn how to effectively relate to each of my students on his or her own terms.

"The deepest principle in human nature is the craving to be appreciated."
—William James

In the process of creating a system to categorize my students, I was a bit worried that people might not want to hear that they have a fixed type. People might resist the notion that they experience the world through one internal lens that never changes no matter how they change and develop throughout their lives.

But if we believe what William James says is true, that humans crave, above all, to be appreciated, then that means we must know how to relate to another person on his or her own terms. To appreciate someone is to accept who he really is deep down. When we recognize someone's inherent type, this is not to impose limits upon him but to give him dignity. Rather than demanding that someone meet us on our level (or according to our *Life Lens*), we can enter into that person's perspective by seeing his *Life Lens*.

I liken this approach to the relief a person feels when communicating in his native tongue. I am sort of able to speak French, but it requires a tremendous amount of mental energy for me to think of the correct vocabulary and verb conjugations necessary to put a good sentence together, and then another one, and still another one. The energy I have to spend trying to function in a foreign language detracts from whatever activity I'm trying to perform—it's mentally exhausting. Conversely, when I speak in my native tongue, English, I don't have to struggle over linguistic considerations and therefore can devote all of my energy to the given activity. When faced with the dilemma of communicating in a foreign language there are two options:

1. I could become more proficient in French to reduce the amount of mental fatigue I experience.
2. People who wish to communicate with me could enter

into my comfort zone and speak to me in English. The former approach puts the burden of communication on me; the latter puts the burden of communication on the other person.

Who do you think should bear the communication burden in a classroom setting? When teaching, I have unwittingly put my young students in the same uncomfortable predicament of having to expend mental energy becoming more proficient in my language. I now know that the better way lies with me (or any adult in their lives) taking the time to learn how to relate to them on *their* terms, learning *their* language. Children want to please and will learn how to speak the adult's "foreign" language. Over time, however, they may feel unappreciated and misunderstood if the most important people in their life, their parents and teachers, do not come down to meet them, enter into their perspective and acknowledge their *Life Lens*.

Psychologists Karen Horney and Carl Rogers explain the child's view:

"When young children feel insecure about being accepted by their parents, they experience great anxiety. They feel lost and alone in a complicated world. Since they are only a few years old, they can't simply reject their parents and say, 'I think I'll go it alone.' They have to find a way to feel safe and to win their parents over" (Dweck 2008, 225).

When I became a mother, I had the mistaken notion that my daughter would be "like" me. After all, she got half of my genetic material! It took me many years to finally realize that my daughter is quite different from me. We view the world through *different* lenses as a result of our different types. Take, for example, the issue of pace. My pace is very fast, but my daughter's speed is slower. She always felt like I was rushing her through a given activity, which made her feel uncomfortable and stressed. I, on the other hand, thought she was procrastinating and wondered why she couldn't keep up. This is but one example of the friction that can erode the closest relationships and create bitterness and resentment over time if left unchecked. After years of trying to please me, my daughter started to push back, resulting in a lot of pain that could have been avoided if only I had been able to recognize her inherent *Life Lens* type.

I have watched this same scenario play out in my lessons with well-meaning parents who dearly love yet misunderstand their kids. Conflicts during home practice escalate, and the process of trying to learn to play a musical instrument highlights the pre-existing cracks in the parent-child relationship. This tragedy need not occur! My goal is to help eliminate unnecessary misunderstanding and tension between parents and children, and people in general. When *Life Lens* informs the way we relate to each other, communication becomes easy and joy results.

PSYCHOLOGY and *Life Lens*

You may also be wondering how *Life Lens* differs from any other personality assessment. With most personality assessments, a person turns out to be a blend of different characteristics. This is not the case with *Life Lens*. Each person has but one *Life Lens*. Many factors influence personality, but underlying each personality variation is one unchanging lens through which the person views the world. *Life Lens* is identifiable in very young children all the way through adulthood.

Psychology deals with the mind and mental processes, which can and do change, like the software that runs on our computers. Software often needs updates. Sometimes we discontinue using one type of software altogether in favor of another type that works better for us. Psychology and personality change and evolve, and many factors contribute to personality such as birth order, family upbringing, and relationship with parents (or lack thereof).

Life Lens resides somewhere deeper than our conscious minds. It's like the hardware that comes with the computer from the factory. *Life Lens* is with you long before you even have the capacity to articulate how you feel and is always on display if you know what it looks like. I know because in my work with young children I've been able to see *Life Lens* very early. One toddler wants to run around and climb, while another wants to carefully push all the same-colored stools together. Beyond being incredibly cute, the toddlers' behaviors reveal important *Life Lens* clues even though they are not able to fill out a questionnaire or tell you what they're doing.

Life Lens principles have far-reaching implications beyond the arena of the Suzuki method of music instruction. If you are not involved with Suzuki, or music at all, the *Life Lens* principles can easily be adapted to your specific activities. Just as Agatha Christie's seminal detective Jane Marple solved complex riddles by comparing a new scenario with situations she had previously encountered in her small village, I am using Suzuki guitar lessons as my familiar, small village. The principles I lay out are universal—they will lead to more harmony and less tension between parents and children, co-workers, team-mates, and people in general. All *Life Lens* types have wonderful merits as well as potential pitfalls. I truly believe that we, as human beings, will benefit from the full spectrum of our collective potential when we learn how each *Life Lens* functions. You don't need a complicated test or any special training to recognize the seven different *Life Lens* types. Learning to discern *Life Lens* is a completely organic process that is easy to learn. Let's get started!

Chapter 1: SEEING THE LIGHT—NINE WINDOWS

Life Lens type is analyzed through nine separate aspects, or windows, which in combination determine the color of a person's lens. As components of *Life Lens*, these are fixed and remain consistent:

1. LEARNING STYLE
2. THINKING STYLE
3. VERBAL EXPRESSIVENESS
4. PACE
5. TEMPORAL ORIENTATION
6. TIME vs. SPACE AWARENESS
7. TIME PATIENCE / TIME URGENCY
8. MOTIVATION
9. RESISTANCE

Life Lens types are named after the colors of the visible spectrum—RED, ORANGE, YELLOW, GREEN, BLUE, INDIGO, and VIOLET. The next chapter will describe each *Life Lens* color in detail, but first we will break down how each window is reflected in the seven colors of *Life Lens* by examining observable behavior through examples. As I describe the nine windows, you may want to turn to the table at the end of chapter two to see the whole *Life Lens* picture—if at this moment you can't wait to flip through the book to find that master table without reading anything else, you're most likely BLUE or VIOLET!

LEARNING STYLES—AUDITORY, KINESTHETIC, VISUAL

A learning style refers to the way a person best receives new information, or the manner of input. The three learning styles are:

Auditory: learns best by *hearing*

Kinesthetic: learns best by *doing*

Visual: learns best by *seeing*

Though all of us are capable of learning via all learning styles, each of us learns *easiest* and *best* with one particular style. Learning style is akin to one's native language. Since a person functions most efficiently in their primary language, it follows that teaching new information according to a person's best learning style will enable them to learn more quickly and easily. Let's look at examples of learning styles as seen in the different *Life Lens* types.

AUDITORY (ORANGE)

Auditory learners do best when they say or sing out loud the material they need to learn. ORANGE, the only auditory learner of all seven colors, prefers that you just TELL them what to do. And when they hear themselves vocalize a task, this also helps them learn efficiently. For instance, if I want to teach a young ORANGE guitar student the four steps of correct guitar posture in her chair, I would first TELL her the four steps, and then I would have her SAY the steps out loud while doing them:

"1. Take a bow."

"2. Feet apart."

"3. Sit and rocket blastoff."

"4. Close the door, heart to heart."

A more advanced ORANGE auditory learner might SAY and PLAY tricky spots in a guitar piece. For example, she might say aloud the right-hand finger cues as she plays, or the note names, or postural details . . . anything!

The co-founder of the Suzuki Guitar pedagogy William Kossler sums up this principle: "From the student's mouth, to their ears, to their brain" (W. Kossler, pers. comm.). It matters not what you are teaching to an auditory learner. Just remember, if they say it, they will learn it!

KINESTHETIC (RED, GREEN)

Kinesthetic learners need a tactile component involved in their task. They learn by DOING. Of course, playing a musical instrument *is* a tactile endeavor, but how we learn the skills to play the instrument is the issue. The four steps of correct posture mentioned previously exemplify learning by DOING. The students not only see what to do and say what to do, but they actually DO it. Kinesthetic learners learn a lot through trial and error. These resilient people view failure as a learning experience. As RED Thomas Edison famously said, "I haven't failed. I've just found 10,000 ways that won't work" (Garcia 2013).

When working with kinesthetic learners, a teacher must keep in mind that these students' resiliency is both a blessing and a curse. Because they love trial and error and will repeat a task consistently, it is almost more important for these learners to get it right the first time. I try to give my students lots of opportunities for trial while eliminating the possibility for error since the physical nature of their learning will deepen the errors, making them even more difficult to correct later on.

VISUAL (BLUE, VIOLET, YELLOW, INDIGO)

My BLUE daughter helped me realize that as a visual learner she worked most efficiently when I could demonstrate what she should do on her violin before she attempted the task herself. She would watch and then copy what I did. Unfortunately, my violin skills are limited, so most of the time I could not show her what to do, so instead of showing, I resorted to *telling* her what to do. Though she's able to function with spoken instructions, it isn't her most efficient method of learning. After a while, too much talking would annoy her — I would devolve into the teacher from the *Peanuts* cartoon who only uttered, "Blah, blah, blah, blah, blahhhh." Worse yet, as a RED person, I talk a lot! My words, no matter how insightful and loving, were not received well at all. They were like static interfering with her learning process. This created tension and often resulted in arguments. At the time I thought we were fighting about violin practice, but I now understand that my failure to recognize and respect my daughter's preferred visual learning style was the real issue.

Now, whenever I have a BLUE student I show more and tell less. In fact, by sitting next to the student so that they can see my hands, I've learned that I need very few words during a lesson. If they need help, I adjust their hand position. They see what to do and then do it. Imagine the person's relief when the constant flow of noisy static in the background that inhibits their concentration is finally turned off. This is the experience of a BLUE visual learner allowed to learn visually without the background noise of constant verbal instructions.

ALL VISUAL LEARNERS ARE NOT THE SAME

The big surprise came when I found that there are *different kinds* of visual learners:

1. Those who prefer to watch someone do the task and then copy them.
2. Those who prefer to look at written material.

BLUE and VIOLET fall into the former category, while YELLOW and INDIGO are among the latter. At first, I thought all visual learners were like my BLUE daughter, but I quickly found that the "watch-and-copy" strategy didn't work as well with YELLOW and INDIGO students. Read on for more about the distinctions among visual learners.

VISUAL WATCH and COPY (BLUE, VIOLET)

Blue Linear

I've already described the BLUE visual watch-and-copy learner who can simply watch what someone else is doing and then copy them. If you show BLUEs examples, they will thrive. Show them the correct way to do it and also show them the incorrect way so that they can compare their work to both. BLUE students excel when they can see video of what to do.

Violet Versatile

VIOLET is also a watch-and-copy learner, same as BLUE. The difference is that VIOLET thinks in a more spatial manner and understands written diagrams, floor plans, and maps very well, whereas BLUE does not. VIOLET reads every spare moment for fun and, therefore, also handles written linear information well. VIOLET is versatile and is the only *Life Lens* that functions equally well in any modality of visual learning, though visual watch and copy is the most efficient and best way for them to learn.

VISUAL WRITTEN (YELLOW, INDIGO)

Yellow Diagrammatic

YELLOW thrives when given written diagrams of the material containing all the information needed to do the task. A dramatic example of the YELLOW visual written diagrammatic style appeared in my four-year-old student Gary. We were learning a rhythm (ti-ti-ti-ti, ta, ta) by saying words that naturally mirror the rhythm (wa-ter-mel-on jel-ly). I asked Gary to clap after me, and I clapped the syllables while saying the words aloud: "Wa-ter-mel-on jel-ly." He shook his head, no. I demonstrated again. This time, Gary not only shook his head no, but he also leaned back on his stool as if trying to get as far away from me as possible without leaving his seat. Watching and copying was obviously not working! Then, I reached into my bag and showed Gary this visual:

Instantly, Gary smiled and clapped the rhythm! Eureka! I showed him five other rhythm picture cards, and he happily clapped them all. Far from his earlier posture of resistance, now Gary was smiling and cooperating. The only difference between resistance and cooperation was the way in which I presented the information. YELLOW learns best when given a visual written diagram. I term them *visual written diagrammatic* learners.

Indigo Linear

Energized by my new discovery with YELLOW Gary, I made guitar fretboard diagram charts (see the picture below) to use with my visual written learners. Imagine my surprise when INDIGO Greg looked at my fretboard diagram and announced, "I don't really understand that." This was my first inkling that a further difference existed between different types of visual written learners.

After much experimentation, I realized that INDIGO students do not learn best by seeing a diagram but prefer written information presented in a linear way. They learn best when they can see the information written in a step-by-step manner, rather than in a diagram where all the information is spread out in space. Below is an example of the exact same information shown above on the fretboard in diagram form but now rewritten in a linear presentation.

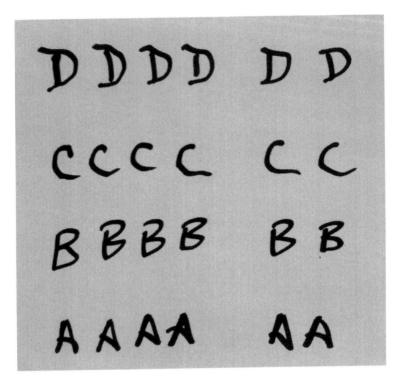

INDIGO Greg responded immediately by playing the notes because he had seen the information written in the way he understood best.

When I found myself puzzling over how to apply this strategy to technical problems my INDIGO students were having, I consulted an expert—INDIGO Abby, the twelve-year-old sister of two of my guitar students. I asked Abby to create a visual to help teach a student how to stop cutting off his notes. I wanted the student to let the notes he played ring, but the INDIGO student kept stopping them by touching the string. Abby, though not a guitar student, understood the objective and in a few minutes had come up with this picture. Even though it is a drawing, notice the linear (left to right, step-by-step) story-telling quality of the explanation:

"The wall is blocking the sound so that the two kids can't talk. This is like your finger. It is blocking the sound when it touches the string. If your finger doesn't touch the string, you will get much better sound, just like if you took the wall away." Artwork by Abigail Knight

At my lesson with the INDIGO student who had been cutting off notes, I pulled out my secret weapon: Abby's drawing. I showed it to the boy. He read it in about thirty seconds, said "Hmm," and then proceeded to play his piece without cutting off a single note! Amazing.

Once again I had witnessed the dramatic difference of presenting information according to the student's *Life Lens* type. It saved time and effort and eliminated frustration.

The differences in the four subsets of visual learners might seem difficult to grasp right away, but when you see how these learning styles relate to the different *thinking styles* of their *Life Lens* types, the differences will become more obvious.

THINKING STYLES—LINEAR, GLOBAL, CIRCULAR

A thinking style refers to how a person processes information. After a new concept is presented, a person's thinking style determines how the information is best retained and understood.

LINEAR (RED, ORANGE, INDIGO)
A person with a *linear* thinking style processes information one thing at a time in a step-by-step manner. Though RED, ORANGE, and INDIGO all process information in a linear way, they will do it at very different speeds and with very different motivations, as you will see later in the chapter.

GLOBAL (GREEN)
Global thinkers process many things simultaneously, considering all the information all at once and not in any particular order. They need to consider all the components to understand the big picture. GREEN people exemplify this energetic thinking style, making them both powerful and easily distractible.

LINEAR-GLOBAL (BLUE)
It might seem counterintuitive to combine these thinking styles, but BLUE absolutely needs to learn new information this way. They like to first absorb the information broken down step-by-step in a linear manner. Then, once they have internalized

and understood the material, they can think about all of it and apply it in a global, big picture way.

GLOBAL-LINEAR (YELLOW)

YELLOW is exactly the opposite of BLUE. This person needs all the information for a project up front. YELLOW must first grasp the big picture of the given task; then, once they know all the various parts of the project, they can process each one in-depth in a linear fashion.

CIRCULAR (VIOLET)

Circular thinking is always spiraling back. In conversation, VIOLET is compelled to come back to any open conversation threads and close them, and there are usually a number of threads intertwining in these conversations. Think of it like the computer game Tetris. Circular thinkers are always a few steps ahead, arranging and connecting ideas and objects in their mind as they go, to fit them into a bigger picture.

VERBAL EXPRESSIVENESS— "First Talkers"

How children express themselves says a lot about their *Life Lens*, but the nature of their expressiveness is most readily apparent when in a group setting or with a stranger. In the beginning of my work developing *Life Lens* diagnostics, I used to ask parents if they thought their children were "verbal expressive extraverts." Much to my surprise, almost all parents said yes! Why? Because children talk a lot to their parents at home. However, they might not talk at all when in front of a group, especially with people they don't know. Therefore, to explain how people express themselves in a group or stranger setting, I stopped using the term "extravert" and switched to the term "first talker" to describe the verbal expressive person who talks first in a group of strangers (Introvert and Extravert 2014).

Identifying first talkers is a powerful diagnostic tool, because they are always either RED or GREEN. When I am conducting a workshop in a new setting, I notice the people who come right up to me and start talking. They are either RED or GREEN. (The ones who approach me in the hallway during the bathroom break are most likely BLUE. They don't want to risk asking a question in front of the whole group, but they are curious, so they wait until the break when it's a lower risk opportunity to ask their question. But more on BLUE later . . .)

It's easy to identify "first talker" children. At the Brooklyn Conservatory of Music, part of my work is to interview prospective students and their families for admission to the music program. I am a complete stranger to these children, who are usually between the ages of three and five, so naturally when I first open the office door and go out in the hallway to greet the family and invite them in, most kids are shy or quiet. They don't know me or what is expected or what will happen. I can always tell when I've got a "first talker," though, because the minute I open my door the kid is walking in and talking to me, and I instantly recognize that *this* kid is RED or GREEN. It is then just a matter of determining if the child is strongly opinionated and judgmental (RED) or if he is more interested in getting me to like him (GREEN).

RED and GREEN don't have the market cornered on prolific talking, though. There are other *Life Lens* types who can also take up a lot of air in the room, but the difference is they will not *initiate* the conversation with strangers. VIOLET heads the list, which also includes INDIGO. These *Life Lens* types will do a lot of talking with people they know, or if a stranger initiates conversation with them.

BLUE kids will typically give information when they are asked to but not offer any on their own. YELLOW kids would NEVER be the first to speak in a group of strangers because they have a deep need to see the whole picture and understand the context completely before joining in. ORANGE kids like to be out of the spotlight and fly under the radar, but if they are specifically asked to demonstrate or present something in a group setting, they will rise to the task because of their deep need to be helpful.

PACE

Natural pace is the speed at which a person experiences life. Generally, does the person in question approach day-to-day activities at a fast, medium, or slow speed? Not coincidentally, pace not only describes how fast a person moves through life but also the speed at which he or she makes decisions and approaches work (Gevers, Mohammed, and Baytalskaya 2014).

FAST (RED, GREEN)
It makes sense that the same *Life Lens* types who are "first talkers" would experience life at a fast pace. They don't have time to be introduced before getting the ball rolling!

MEDIUM (BLUE, INDIGO)
BLUE people's need for peace and safety keeps them from being fast-paced, but they still want to move on and get a task done, so their pace is medium fast. INDIGO people also work at

a medium fast pace, even though their motivation is "bigger, better, farther, faster," because of their steady linear thinking styles.

SLOW (ORANGE, YELLOW, VIOLET)

It takes time to do one thing at a time well, and that is how the ORANGE monotasker goes about things. YELLOW people are even slower because of their deep need to gather all the facts related to a project before making a single move. VIOLET is slowest of all, since every piece of a project, every bit of information being learned, must fit into a beautiful and cohesive whole before VIOLET can call it complete.

TEMPORAL ORIENTATION

"Temporal orientation" is a term coined by time researchers to describe how a person responds (or doesn't respond) to deadlines. Temporal orientation also reveals the conditions for a person's maximum release of creativity and best work. The three types of temporal orientation are *deadline action*, *early action*, and *steady action* (Mohammed and Harrison 2003). If you ask people to work in a way that is contrary to their *Life Lens* type, it will diminish their creativity and adversely affect the quality of their work on a project.

DEADLINE (RED, YELLOW)

Deadline-action individuals don't start working until close to the deadline, and they finish just before the deadline. They also need a deadline to motivate them (Mohammed and Harrison 2003). RED waits until the last minute and easily handles tasks by priority, always aware of each one's due date. YELLOW is so focused on gathering all the possible information and making sure it is accurate, that there absolutely must be a hard deadline or the project will never be finished.

EARLY (GREEN, BLUE)

Early action individuals start working immediately after the project is assigned and finish well in advance of the due date (Mohammed and Harrison 2003). GREEN people work best, at their peak of creativity, when they start a project right away and finish it early. BLUE people will usually get the work done ahead of the deadline on their own schedule. Though young children will need adult guidance for setting up a schedule for their work, they do not like to feel pressured and will, as they grow older, prefer to make their own schedule for completing a project or assignment.

STEADY (ORANGE, INDIGO, VIOLET)

Steady-action individuals start working at the beginning of the project and steadily work every day up until the end of the project (Mohammed and Harrison 2003). ORANGE students never enjoy pressure to get something done, no matter what the assignment or task. And although INDIGO likes to race the clock when it comes to finishing short, succinct tasks, when a task or project requires more than one class to accomplish, INDIGO favors working steadily toward the due date and finishing right before the deadline. Slow meticulous VIOLET needs all the time allotted for a given project, so they must begin right away and work steadily if they are to finish on time. Do not nag them, it will just make them slower.

TIME vs. SPACE AWARENESS

I've noticed that people are usually more attuned to either time or space depending on their *Life Lens*. RED, ORANGE, BLUE, and INDIGO are more time sensitive, whereas YELLOW, GREEN, and VIOLET are space sensitive. Interestingly, the time-sensitive *Life Lens* types experience time quite differently from one another, and, likewise, the space-sensitive *Life Lens* types also have their different concepts of space. It is difficult to explain these differences abstractly, but the examples below should make them clear.

TIME AWARE (RED, ORANGE, BLUE, INDIGO)

RED—*Driven, Internal Awareness*
RED has a strong desire to be on time, hates to be late, and hates it when others are late. They are always aware of time because they have an accurate internal clock — they know how long it will take to do something or get some place, and how much time has passed. Ironically, RED also waits until the last minute to do things, in the deadline-action style. RED suffers from tunnel vision, obsessively working to solve a problem or complete a task to the exclusion of all else. If RED students are in the middle of working on something, it's difficult for them to leave it in order to start something else. RED likes closure. They want to finish and then be able to fully devote themselves to the next thing.

ORANGE—*Steady Monotasker*
ORANGE is also time aware but in a much different way than the driven RED. ORANGE awareness of time centers around consistency. ORANGE students do not respond well if pressured to get something done; they function best when they take a steady-ac-

tion approach, that is, when they work a little bit every day to accomplish a task.

BLUE—*Intuitive*

BLUE experiences time in an intuitive manner. They internally know *when* to do a given thing to get the best outcome. For this reason, the imposition of deadlines on BLUE foments low-grade tension because it messes with BLUE's internal clock. They want to do a task when they want to do it and resent it if you make them do it either sooner or later.

INDIGO—*Beat the Clock*

INDIGO thrives on time pressure and actually enjoys deadlines! They experience time as a challenge and love to beat the clock. To keep INDIGO students from losing interest, simply give them the objective, start the stopwatch, and turn them loose. INDIGO likes to keep moving forward and does not do well with repetitions and monotony.

SPACE AWARE (YELLOW, GREEN, VIOLET)

YELLOW—*Functionality*

Functionality of space means the most to YELLOW. YELLOW is always asking, "Does the space serve its purpose efficiently?" To YELLOW students, "functionality" means having everything they're working on spread out *where they can see it* and use it. All ongoing projects live on their desk until they're completed, not in a filing cabinet, even if the projects take months to finish. It may seem a bit chaotic to an outsider, but YELLOW people know where to find things in the midst of the spread. They do not want their work area disturbed. When they have completed the work they will put things away in an organized manner.

When planning their spaces, YELLOW people also like to research and then diagram or draw a plan for the space before physically adjusting it (i.e., moving furniture, remodeling, gardening). This gives them a chance to visualize the changes and think about all the details before actually changing something.

GREEN—Psychological Common Ground

Just as the sun shines onto the earth and brings everyone into its light, GREEN people radiate their personality outward and draw everyone into their psychological space. The GREEN concept of space is to assimilate everyone into whatever they're doing. GREEN loves to be around people. It follows that their spatial orientation doesn't have anything to do with planning and creating physical, functional space like YELLOW but concerns winning over others to their way of thinking.

VIOLET—Beautiful Ecosystem

What inspires VIOLET? Beauty. The VIOLET concept of space is everything in its place functioning as a perfect whole. VIOLET craves a complete ecosystem. They want to have perfection, whether it's coloring a picture, arranging furniture in a room, or creating a work schedule. In any and every endeavor VIOLET wants a complete and finished product where every component functions beautifully and perfectly together. Creating such quality takes time. VIOLET people do not respond well to nagging. Give them plenty of time and don't rush them. They do their best work when they are *inspired,* not when they are pressured.

TIME PATIENCE/TIME URGENCY

If given a choice between getting something done by a deadline even if it means taking shortcuts on quality or spending longer to get the project done right even if it's late, time-patient individuals choose the latter. Though aware of time and deadlines, the time-patient person's desire to get a job done right trumps getting it done on time. Time-urgent people are just the opposite. The time-urgent person will get the work done by the deadline even if quality suffers because getting it done on time takes priority.

PATIENT (ORANGE, YELLOW, VIOLET)

ORANGE does not like pressure and is rather content to steadily work on one thing at a time and do it well. YELLOW people are so focused on gathering every detail and making sure their work is accurate, they prefer to sacrifice meeting a deadline than having their work be incomplete. VIOLET is patient almost to a fault. The perfection of the work is of utmost importance and will never be sacrificed to meet a deadline.

URGENT (RED, GREEN, BLUE, INDIGO)

It makes perfect sense that RED would be time urgent, but what about BLUE or INDIGO? BLUE's intuitive sense of time plays into their need to get their work done by the deadline. INDIGO loves to beat the clock and loves to plan out and organize multiple projects according to deadlines. This is how their time urgency plays into their *steady-action style*—INDIGO is planning how to get everything done on time. GREEN wants to finish on time so that everyone is in harmony, but they must be careful they don't employ the it's-the-thought-that-counts mentality, or the quality of their work may suffer.

MOTIVATION and RESISTANCE

Each *Life Lens* has an overall defining motivation, and each type also has unique ways of displaying resistance to learning something new. As a teacher or parent, it pays to keep in mind the primary motivations of your children and be able to recognize the signs of resistance in their different *Life Lens* types. We will explore motivations and resistance signs in the next chapter. They can also be found in the master table at the end of chapter two.

Chapter 2:
THE COLORS OF *Life Lens*

In this chapter, we will explore each of the seven *Life Lens* types in depth and detail with lots of examples and strategies. But first, let's take a minute to visualize the thinking processes of the different *Life Lens* styles, with marbles representing new ideas.

A MARBLE ANALOGY

RED *RAPID FIRE, RELOAD, RAPID FIRE*

If the RED thought process was a tube full of marbles, each marble would represent a task to be completed, prioritized by due date. RED fires through the marbles like bullets in a gun, one after the other in rapid succession, and then moves on to the next tube of tasks. RED people may reload the marbles and revisit each project as they work simultaneously on multiple projects, but while they are working on each tube they have tunnel vision.

If you want RED to get something done, give her a deadline. Otherwise, your task won't make it into her mental marble queue. RED people become more creative as the deadline approaches. They are time urgent and *will* finish their work just under the wire.

ORANGE *ONE AT A TIME*

Imagine yourself slowly rolling marbles to ORANGE, one at a time. ORANGE will take plenty of time to pick up each marble and put it in the proper category. ORANGE people process best when they handle one thing at a time. If the marbles come at them too fast or if two or more marbles come at them at once, ORANGE people get overwhelmed and may whine, complain, or cry, a sure sign that they are feeling overwhelmed, either by time pressure or by having to multitask.

YELLOW RESEARCH and UNDERSTAND

YELLOW wants to see all of the marbles initially and then analyze each one individually in depth. What is the marble made of—minerals, rosin, glass, wood, plastic? Is it handmade or machine made? What is the diameter of each marble? Are the marbles perfectly round or are there inconsistencies? What is the history of each marble? YELLOW people will research until they are satisfied and will not necessarily *do* anything with the marbles until they are asked.

GREEN SOCIAL ROLLER

GREEN people want to get all the marbles all at once. Once they have all the marbles, they can then call their friends to come over and play with them. They want to get people involved with their marbles, the more the merrier!

BLUE CATCH and RELEASE

BLUE will examine each marble one by one, and then once all the marbles are in hand BLUE will come up with a plan to use the marbles in a way that no one else thought of. BLUE will market the marbles and release them to a bigger audience, usually benefitting many and making a profit. BLUE also instinctively knows which particular marble to play at any given time for the optimum result.

INDIGO BIGGER, BETTER, FARTHER, FASTER

INDIGO will go through all the marbles one at a time, organize them, and then create three times the amount of amazing things as the non-INDIGO, such as marble coasters, marble toys, marble jewelry, marble salt and pepper shakers, marble sculptures, and more.

To perfectly explain the INDIGO thought process, pictures speak louder than words. Look at the following photos of burrs. You know, *burrs* . . . those annoying prickly things that fall off of trees. Have any of you ever given more than a moment's thought to what to do with a bunch of burrs? I didn't think so. INDIGO Tallulah beautifully illustrates the "bigger, better, farther, faster" principle. Rather than becoming annoyed with all the prickly burrs at the park, Tallulah collected them and then crafted them into a hat for her friend!

Photos by Jason Gonsky, used with permission

VIOLET ECOSYSTEM

VIOLET needs a lot of time to carefully examine each marble and think about how they will all fit together in a beautiful, harmonious whole where each marble can function perfectly and also look beautiful. Will this blue marble work better *here* or *there?* This level of beauty and perfection takes time to achieve. VIOLET may have to sit with the marbles for a while, just examining each one and noticing how they feel and how they roll. My VIOLET friend Julianne said, "If someone handed me a tube of marbles, the first thing I would do is roll them back and forth in the tube and enjoy the sound and feeling of them bumping into each other. Rolling them onto the floor, I would make sure they didn't roll away from me. Then I would play with them—primarily as a physical sensation—feel them roll on the floor under my hands, see how they bump off of other objects, notice if the floor was level. I'd look through them into the light. It would be a very physical experience. I'm not sure I would need them to function perfectly . . . the function is to roll them, so they're already doing that. But they do look pretty, and I would enjoy looking at them all."

I found "marble art" online—a full portrait of LeBron James made out of marbles (later I learned that they are actually Skittles!), and although I can't confirm that artist Andrei Bilan who created this amazing likeness of Lebron James is a VIOLET, I certainly wouldn't be surprised if he were! Each and every piece is positioned perfectly to create a beautiful picture, a complete ecosystem.

THE COLORS OF *Life Lens*

Now that you have a glimpse into what differentiates the seven different *Life Lens* types and what aspects we must consider when determining *Life Lens*, let's look at each color in depth and really get to know the spectrum. At the end of the chapter, there is a reference table that lays out each *Life Lens* color and its nine windows.

RED

Behavioral Characteristics

- Tightly focused
- Have tunnel vision
- Task and goal oriented
- First talkers
- Strong sense of right and wrong
- Defensive about their rights (sometimes to the detriment of their responsibilities)
- Quick to judge *everything*
- Highly opinionated
- Love to solve problems—can always find something to improve
- Passionate
- Intense
- Risk takers
- Respond well to strong leadership (resist weak leadership)
- Make great leaders
- Embrace new challenges
- Understand abstract concepts

- See patterns and make connections
- Highly competitive
- Visionary: Long-range vision
- Creative and inventive
- Thrive on pressure/deadlines
- Kinesthetic learners
- Linear thinkers
- Very fast-paced; quick decision makers
- Time aware

RED is like an engine that never stops. RED people go full speed into whatever they are doing. They are all in! RED is intense, emotional, and passionate. RED experiences life at a very fast pace, the fastest pace of all. As children, they like to run, jump, and climb things. They are movers and shakers. RED makes fast decisions. They learn by *doing*, their best learning is kinesthetic.

RED's mind is constantly moving, as is his mouth (well, maybe not constantly, but RED talks a lot!). RED fearlessly speaks to anyone about anything. As a RED baby in the stroller, I used to say "hi" to every person we passed on the sidewalk.

RED has a vision. They have clear ideas about what they want, how it should be, how it should work, and how it can be better. They understand how doing "X" now will have a huge effect on what happens far into the future.

RED students enjoy doing puzzles and inventing things. They like new technology and ideas. They take big risks. RED is task oriented. They love to fix things and solve problems. RED is wildly creative. Not knowing what they're doing does not deter them; they will figure it out! RED is fearless by nature and not afraid to try new things to achieve a goal.

RED is made to lead and responds well to strong leadership (and not well to weak leadership).

RED people are tightly focused. When they are engaged in a project, that's all they can think about until they have finished because they like closure. For instance, if a RED child is fully engrossed in playing with her toys, she won't want to stop to come to dinner. "How can I eat when I'm in the middle of THIS?!" she thinks. The fact that they need to eat and that Mom will be mad if they don't run downstairs to dinner fade in the background of finishing what they're doing with their toys. REDs are driven to complete their mission.

RED is highly competitive about everything! They enjoy competition and want to win. RED thrives under pressure. RED needs a challenge to stay motivated. RED also needs a goal, make that a BIG goal, and an impossible goal is even better! RED will rise to the occasion.

RED is ideologically motivated. When they believe in something, REDs will not back down, even in the face of adversity. RED constantly judges right/wrong, good/bad. They make instant evaluations of pretty much everything, constantly. RED people are extremely sensitive when they feel that they have been wronged, and they are passionate about both *being* right and their perceived rights.

KINESTHETIC LEARNERS

RED learns best by doing. In the process of doing, or trying to do a given activity, RED will make lots of mistakes. This does not discourage them at all because they learn from their mistakes. There is no such thing as failure in the mind of a RED. The secret to helping RED learn anything is to include a kinesthetic component in the activity. Ask yourself, how can I help them *do*? If you can find a way to incorporate "trial" and eliminate "error" in the process, you will streamline RED's learning curve immensely. I will go into detail on best practices for working with kinesthetic learners in chapter four: Strategies for Success.

LINEAR PROCESSORS

RED sees patterns, makes connections, and processes information, including the symbolic and abstract, in a logical and linear fashion. Linear processing also explains why in the course of solving one problem, RED can inadvertently create other problems. Though this might upset those around them, REDs don't mind creating more problems. They just think, "Oh good! More problems to solve!" Arthur Burk likes to recount the story of groundbreaking scientist George Washington Carver, who is a perfect example of RED's linear thinking (Burk 2000). When Carver learned that planting peanuts produced nitrogen in the soil, he passionately shared this new information with all the farmers in the area. Eureka! He had solved the problem of how to enrich the depleted soil! The farmers, acting on Carver's research, planted peanut seeds and in the course of time had a massive crop. The only problem was there was *no* market for peanuts! What were they going to do with a crop that no one wanted? Carver's employer, Booker T. Washington, president of the newly formed Tuskegee Institute, was none too pleased with the complaints of the farmers. He didn't realize that this situation would provide the perfect playing field for RED Carver to solve the new problem and create a market for peanuts. Not only did Carver invent peanut butter (one of the best inventions ever), but he came up with 105 food recipes that used peanuts AND 100 products made with peanuts, including cosmetics, dyes, paints, plastics, gasoline, and nitroglycerine! There. Problem solved.

FAST PACE

RED experiences life at the fastest tempo of all the *Life Lens* types. RED thinks fast, acts fast, moves fast, and then goes on to conquer the next challenge. RED pace is akin to an all-out sprint.

TIME AWARE

When it comes to time and space, RED is time aware. RED hates to be late and hates it when others are late. RED people's internal clock tells them how much time has passed and when they need to move on to the next thing. Ironically, RED also waits until the last minute to do things, in the *deadline-action* style. They wait until close to the deadline to begin, and somehow their creativity peaks as the deadline approaches. They work like crazy to meet the deadline and finish the task just under the wire. Perhaps RED waits until the last minute due to their linear thinking style—they like to finish what they're working on and intuitively know when they have to begin the next task in order to finish on time, even if it's at the last minute, as if the to-do list is marbles in a tube in their minds. They handle tasks by priority, always maintaining an awareness of each one's due date, as they pop out each marble, usually rapid fire.

RED suffers from tunnel vision, obsessively working to solve a problem or complete a task to the exclusion of all else. They want to finish and have resolution and then be able to fully devote themselves to the next thing. Because RED people are also *time urgent*, they are willing to interrupt their trial-and-error process in order to get a task done on time. Quality may suffer as a result, since RED takes pleasure in learning from mistakes.

As a child I remember how annoyed I felt when I had to stop playing with my action figures in order to do a chore. My mom constantly heard things from me like, "In a minute!" or, "I'll do it later," because I didn't want to stop what I was doing prematurely. This usually resulted in Mom yelling at me until I capitulated and did the necessary task. Mom coined a term to describe my propensity for getting things done at the last minute. She would chide, "Don't be such a minuteman, Michele!" never appreciating that I always *did* manage to get things done by the deadline, which I thought was a good thing! My deadline-action, time-aware style created quite a bit of tension between us.

PITFALLS

RED's strengths can also manifest as unpleasant behavior. They are keenly attuned to their "rights" and get very angry when they feel that their rights or their friends' rights (or *anyone's* rights that they care about) have been violated. RED can also be extremely defensive when confronted. They want to be right and don't like it when someone points out that they're wrong.

RED is either loved or hated. Their passionate intensity and insistence that they are right combined with their quick tongue can get RED in trouble, especially when others don't see things their way. They value being right over maintaining their relationships. Sometimes RED people are hated for acting obnoxious, opinionated, unyielding, or belligerent. RED can also be surly or bitter. RED people remember everyone who has slighted them, so they need to actively practice forgiveness to guard against bitterness.

RED people hold themselves to a high standard, so they are hard on themselves and often treat others just as harshly. Being harsh is normal for RED, so it doesn't occur to them that others do not experience life the same way. RED types can be depressed when they fail to live up to their own high standards.

MOTIVATION and RESISTANCE

RED is motivated by solving problems. If they feel they don't have a solution or some sort of strategy to proceed, they may procrastinate. RED students also get defensive when they don't want to do something. Defensiveness can manifest in arguments and escalate into aggressive or combative behavior. Because RED people tend to think they're right, they are willing to go down swinging to defend their "rightness."

COLOR	Learning Style	Thinking Style	Verbal Expressive-ness	Natural Pace	Temporal Orientation	Time/ Space	Time Urgent/ Time Patient	Motivation	Resistance
RED	Kines-thetic	Linear	First Talker	Fastest	Deadline action	Time: internal aware-ness	Urgent	Solving Problems	Defensive

ORANGE

Behavioral Characteristics

- Do not draw attention to themselves
- Don't want to lead, though they are highly competent and capable
- Though they don't like to be put on the spot in a group, their desire to be helpful will override their natural disinclination to lead in a group setting
- Get along well with others; great teammates
- Can concentrate for extended periods of time and focus when they have a **clear objective** (one point to focus on)
- Monotaskers
- Competitive in sports and board games, but not in other areas of life
- Strong loyalty to family, eager to please their parents
- Like to collect stuff (cards, action figures, silly bandz, etc.)
- Not always organized
- Dependable and trustworthy
- Don't have their own agenda, they support the agenda of others
- Obedient and trusting
- Follow directions to a T
- Auditory learners
- Linear thinkers
- Slow decision makers
- Motivated by helping others, not for themselves. In fact, self-recognition may be demotivating.

- At their core, they want to make a difference in someone else's life—this gives them a great sense of fulfillment. It is crucial to TELL them that what they're doing really IS helpful to someone else, even if it's just to you, the parent or teacher.

ORANGE is steady and dependable. They follow directions to a T and are trusting and trustworthy.

ORANGE people work best on one thing at a time; they like to be told what to do. ORANGE *monotasks* (the opposite of multitasking). ORANGE students find it overwhelming when they have more than one thing to focus on at a time. Give them a clear objective and they will do excellent work. Overwhelm them and they will whine, complain, or cry. Their natural pace is slow, and they do not like to be put under pressure.

ORANGE loves to collect things and organize them: cards, stickers, action figures, or dolls. They learn best when they can accumulate objects.

ORANGE is not verbally expressive in a group. They do not like calling attention to themselves, but they can be quite talkative with family and friends. ORANGE people don't have their own agenda and are excellent listeners.

ORANGE people want to help others and know that they made a difference in someone else's life. This is what most motivates ORANGE. They don't draw attention to themselves and don't like to lead, though they are competent and capable. ORANGE naturally possesses a joyful disposition and gets along well with everyone. ORANGE competes in sports and board games but not in other areas of life.

ORANGE children like to crawl under things. They enjoy making tents out of blankets and forts out of boxes. You might find them hiding under the table or under the bed. ORANGE children also talk or sing to themselves while they play, an example of their auditory *Life Lens*.

AUDITORY LEARNERS

ORANGE students learn best by hearing instructions or when they repeat aloud to themselves what they're trying to learn. ORANGE can learn *anything* easily by saying it out loud—vocabulary words, multiplication tables, formulae, theorems, foreign languages—anything.

LINEAR PROCESSORS

ORANGE processes new information one item at a time, step by step in a linear manner. ORANGE children enjoy putting things into categories. For instance, if they're collecting colored candy, they might enjoy counting how many reds, blues, greens, and oranges they have accumulated. Accumulation is a key principle for ORANGE. They like to mark successful learning tasks with one collector's item. It almost doesn't matter what the collector's item is: candy, popcorn kernels, pennies, stickers, rubber bands, anything. ORANGE likes to collect and accumulate. They might not always get the big picture, but they're great at following directions.

ORANGE likes to be told what to do, one thing at a time. Returning to the marble analogy, when you give ORANGE a marble, he will put it in his bag. The marble is the assigned task, and putting the marble into the bag means that ORANGE has mastered or completed that particular task. Then and only then are they ready for the next marble.

Not surprisingly, the implementation of the marble metaphor is also a successful teaching strategy when working with ORANGE. Give them an empty bag and let them put in one piece of candy, or one kernel of popcorn, or one *something* for each successful task or repetition of a task. ORANGE will joyfully execute learning tasks when the possibility exists for physically accumulating something, even as they are mentally mastering skills, one at a time.

SLOW PACE

ORANGE experiences life at a slow pace. They like to master one thing at a time before moving on to the next task, and it takes time to process each thing. They work best with a *steady-action* deadline style, beginning a project when it is assigned and working steadily until the due date. Putting pressure on ORANGE to work faster only stresses them out. Don't rush them! Pressure will not increase their work speed.

TIME AWARE

ORANGE is time aware and time patient. If given a choice between getting something done by a deadline but having to take short-cuts on quality and spending longer to get it done right, ORANGE would choose the latter. They are aware of time and deadlines, but the desire to do something well trumps getting it done on time. And the fact that they need to do one thing at a time means they will not be able to multitask to get their tasks finished, so a steady-action style, starting early and maintaining a steady pace through the deadline will enable ORANGE people to do their best work.

PITFALLS

ORANGE tends to notice what they didn't do well versus what they *did* do well. They can default to feeling bad about themselves, and if the going gets tough, ORANGE may be inclined to give up. They do not like to lead! Even though they are competent, ORANGE people prefer to maintain a low profile rather than assert themselves or take charge, even when what they have to bring to the table is sorely needed. Because they like to follow instructions, ORANGE can flounder when tasks are unclear or when they are required to impose their own structure on unstructured tasks (i.e., they are in a position where no one is telling them what to do).

ORANGE wants to help whenever possible, which can make them vulnerable to being taken advantage of. ORANGE, motivated by helping others, is also susceptible to saying "yes" to too many things and then feeling overwhelmed by all the things on their plate and their slow pace finishing tasks. ORANGE must guard against discouragement and feeling like a victim.

MOTIVATION and RESISTANCE

ORANGE people are motivated by helping others. They will do anything to support their friends or teachers when asked to do so. Because they are monotaskers, too many things all at once overwhelm ORANGE. In ORANGE students this usually manifests in whining, crying, or shutting down altogether. It's their way of saying, "I'm overwhelmed by too much to do!" My ORANGE friend Susan explains, "I might cancel a piano lesson because I have been too discouraged to practice after my piano teacher bogs me down with a list of homework tasks. When I tell her that I cannot possibly master two brand-new pieces, review two old pieces, and practice sight-reading in only a week, she still insists, so I end up quitting before I even start practicing. She assumes I am working on multiple pieces at once, but I only work on one thing at a time."

COLOR	Learning Style	Thinking Style	Verbal Expressive-ness	Natural Pace	Temporal Orientation	Time/ Space	Time Urgent/ Time Patient	Motivation	Resistance
Orange	Auditory	Linear	Will talk in agroup by special request	Slow	Steady action	Time: Mono-task	Patient	Helping Others	Whine, Complain, Cry

YELLOW

Behavioral Characteristics

- Very detail-oriented
- Slow-paced; slow decision makers
- Methodical
- Like lists
- Notice details
- Do not like to be put on the spot
- Resist new things—prefer the old thing they've already tested and can do well
- Need plenty of time to practice/learn a new thing
- Neither accept nor reject new information immediately, but must study ALL of the details from many different angles before moving forward with it
- Care deeply about accuracy

- Like to delve deeply into a topic; need to see the complete picture
- Don't anger easily
- Great sense of humor
- Visual learners (written diagram)
- Global thinkers who process in a linear manner
- Spatial
- Don't talk first in a group
- Loyal
- Enjoy factoids
- Non-judgmental

YELLOW notices details that others may miss. YELLOW is never a "first talker." They are quietly watching and taking in all sorts of details. YELLOW children may want to stay close to their mom or dad in a new situation. They like to see what's happening first and get the lay of the land before they know whether or not they want to enter in and participate. They neither accept nor reject a new thing until they've had time to see it and test it out for themselves.

Accuracy matters to YELLOW. They don't care how long it takes for them to complete a given task; they care about doing the task *correctly.* For example, our YELLOW kitchen designer was deeply concerned to know the exact width of the trim around our door so that she would know whether to use a 5/16" or 3/16" spacer for the new pull-out spice rack. Meetings with her would take hours due to her insistence that she know every detail. I found myself thinking about minutia that had never in my whole life entered into my mind. Thanks to the YELLOW thorough mastery of the details, and all of the time we spent discussing them, we now have a beautiful kitchen that functions PERFECTLY! By the way, if the spacer for the spice rack had been too narrow, we would not have been able to open the drawer because it would have run into the door trim!

YELLOW children love to draw and are happy to sit and quietly entertain themselves. I've saved many drawings from my YELLOW students because I know that they took a lot of time and care to make. Usually, the YELLOW child also includes a written description of the picture (just to make sure I under-stand what it is) and their name (just to make sure I know who made it). Here are examples from a four-year-old YELLOW student.

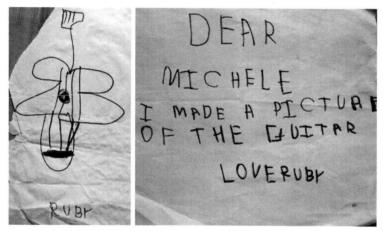

Artwork by Ruby Farmer

VISUAL LEARNERS

YELLOW is a visual learner who learns best when there is a written representation of the concept, preferably in a diagram style. A young YELLOW music student will learn a new rhythm most efficiently if she is able to see a diagram of objects and words that represent the syllabic meter of the rhythm. For example, a repeating triplet might be represented by a picture of two strawberries, with the syllables of the words written out below the picture: "Straw-ber-ry Straw-ber-ry."

An older YELLOW student would best absorb tricky guitar fingering if she sees it written on a fretboard diagram, as shown here. Because YELLOW students are *spatial*, they understand diagrams and schematic drawings.

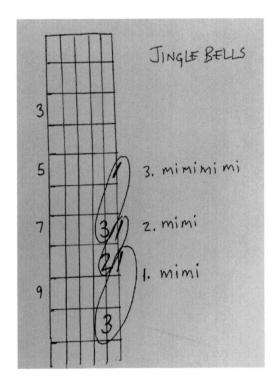

GLOBAL-LINEAR THINKERS

YELLOW students want to collect all the components of new information early on so that they understand how it fits into the big picture, a perfect example of the global thinking style. YELLOW needs *all* the information necessary to put into context with the bigger goal. This is why a YELLOW child wants to observe first before entering into the action. YELLOW adults do not typically watch weekly television shows but instead prefer to wait for the entire series to be completed so they can watch the whole thing all at once to fully understand the big picture. However, once a YELLOW person has the big picture, he will then process each detail step by step in a linear fashion. For example, once I was playing a card game with my student Ruby. The cards featured pictures of all the kings and queens of England. First Ruby wanted to turn over ALL the cards to see the different monarchs—demonstrating her global thinking—so that she could feel satisfied that she had all the information. Once she had seen all the cards, she then proceeded to arrange the monarchs in chronological order, carefully processing all of the information step by step.

SLOW PACE

YELLOW moves at a very slow pace. It takes time for them to process the information and consider all of the details neces-sary to do an excellent job. You can't rush them! They will be finished when they feel satisfied that they have looked at every detail. While YELLOW students need to use the full, allotted time for a project, their creative burst will come right before the deadline. YELLOW people work best under the *deadline-action* approach, or else they will never finish because they are *time patient*.

SPACE AWARE

Functionality of space means the most to YELLOW people. They just want to know: does the space serve its purpose efficiently? It doesn't matter if the space is ugly, cramped, or chaotic. Functionality to YELLOW means having everything they're working on where they can *see* it and access it. They do not want their work area disturbed. When they have completed the work they will put things away in an organized manner.

YELLOW people like to spread out in their workspace. My YELLOW friend Elissah eschews working in her office at her desk, in favor of working at her dining room table. Her office is beautiful! She just prefers working at the table where she can spread out everything that she's working on—laptop, papers, books, magazines—and see it all at once. Elissah says, "I'll bet if I were a musician, I would like to have a nice big space where I could lay out my music, my snack, my instruments, my tools, and myself. I'd like it to feel comfortable, but it might look chaotic to the outside observer."

YELLOW also likes to research and then diagram or plan their space in writing before physically adjusting it (moving furniture, remodeling, gardening). This gives them a chance to visualize the changes and think about all the details before actually changing the space.

PITFALLS

YELLOW moves at a slow pace—it takes time to go into deep

detail and verify the facts of the given project. Their attention to detail can sometimes lead to "analysis paralysis" and make it hard for others to work with them. As an example, while researching my book, I asked some friends to tell me who their favorite fictional character or historical person was when they were growing up. Most people could answer this question on the spot, but my YELLOW friends took *six weeks* to respond. They had to carefully mull over the question; providing an on-the-spot answer was simply not possible for them.

YELLOW needs to be aware that when working with any faster paced peers (RED, GREEN, BLUE, INDIGO) they may become frustrated with each other. YELLOW wants to slow down, and the faster paced person wants to move ahead. YELLOW might have to compromise some of her need for details in order for a project to move forward.

YELLOW's non-judgmental nature can be a blessing and a curse. YELLOW people will never impose their will on another person, even if that person is totally wrong; instead, they might present in great detail all the evidence that makes their case but then, instead of arguing their position, they will just shut down when others don't agree.

MOTIVATION and RESISTANCE

YELLOW students are motivated when they have time to delve deeply into what they're doing and when their work area is completely functional. If they feel they don't have enough time to do an accurate job, they might procrastinate. Parents or teachers of YELLOW students should take care to see to it that YELLOW students can see everything they need around them.

Detail-oriented YELLOW people don't want to forget or overlook *anything*, so their space needs to be arranged accordingly.

YELLOW resists by simply not doing the thing that makes them uncomfortable. They don't usually make a fuss, but will just sit there and not do the task.

COLOR	Learning Style	Thinking Style	Verbal Expressive-ness	Natural Pace	Temporal Orientation	Time/ Space	Time Urgent/ Time Patient	Motivation	Resistance
Yellow	Visual written dia-gramatic	Global -Linear	Never a first talker	Slow	Deadline Action	Space: Func-tionality	Patient	To find functional-ity for each part	Non-partic-ipation

GREEN

Behavioral Characteristics

- First talker
- Visionary
- Life of the party
- Talk to everyone!
- Have their own agenda and want to win you over to it
- Creative
- Curious
- Cause and Effect
- Entrepreneurial
- Care deeply about what other people think of them; want to know they're okay with you
- Like to be around people at all times and don't like to be alone
- May have unrealistic expectations about what can be accomplished in a given time period
- Tend to judge themselves by their own good intentions rather than by what they actually did (It's-the-thought-that-counts mentality)

- Kinesthetic learners
- Spatial awareness
- Enjoy humor and fun
- Very sensitive and can be deeply wounded by criticism from family members. They can, however, handle criticism outside their inner circle, i.e., from teachers
- Global thinkers—very "big picture" and can miss important details
- Fast decision makers

GREEN is a friendly, action-packed, fast-moving, talkative bundle of fun! People love GREEN, and GREEN loves people. GREEN is the quintessential "people person." They don't enjoy being alone for very long. GREEN people are creative visionaries who are all about the big picture and who can mobilize others to make their vision a reality.

Even young GREEN children have their own clear idea about what they want to do (and not do). At every music lesson, a GREEN student will ask to play a specific game or piece of music. GREEN parents do the *same* thing: "Can we do improv today?" or "Can we play pop tunes today?" They have a vision and want to get me on board, the more the merrier!

GREEN people are horizontally focused—they are tuned into everyone around them and want people to like them. GREEN excels at mobilizing others to their cause. They make great entrepreneurs, politicians, and leaders.

KINESTHETIC LEARNERS

GREEN learns by doing. Because they are kinesthetic learners, there is a lot of trial and error involved. GREEN students in a group music class are notorious for "noodling," playing when they're not supposed to. GREEN kids mean no disrespect by playing out of turn; they're simply trying to learn by doing.

GLOBAL THINKERS

The GREEN thinking style is global, they are *so* big picture that important details often elude them. GREEN doesn't mind a visually cluttered workspace, and they actually prefer to have all the information they need right in front of them. It is necessary for GREEN to have each task and the details of *how* the tasks should be accomplished out where they can see them so they don't overlook a key point.

FAST PACE

GREEN experiences life at a very fast pace. They talk fast, think fast, and move fast. GREEN people work best, expressing the most creativity, when they start a project right away and finish it early—this is the *early action* deadline style. If they've procrastinated, GREEN people find themselves functioning in a deadline-action style in which they start late and finish just in time, which is not ideal for GREEN. The most successful GREEN people have learned how to focus early and complete the task ahead of schedule to maximize their creativity.

GREEN people are also time urgent, that is, they care more about finishing a project on time than doing a project well. This doesn't mean that they don't care about quality, but the ultimate challenge for GREEN people is the realization that they must do high-quality work to get a high-quality result. They are tempted to but must not rely on their engaging personality and enthusiasm to guarantee a project's success.

SPACE AWARE

When you engage in any activity with GREEN, you enter into their light. Their concept of space centers around their desire for you to be where they are, to enter into the same *psychological* space. GREEN wants everyone around them joining together on psychological common ground whether it's for two minutes in a grocery line, in a superficial interaction at a restaurant, in a class or work setting, or over an extended period of time.

My GREEN father could have a positive effect on the grumpiest of waiters, so that by the time we left the restaurant they were smiling and friendly. This is an example of GREEN drawing others into their realm. In high school, my GREEN friend Megan was the proverbial life of the party. She had her finger on the pulse of the social calendar and loved bringing people together. She knew where the fun would be, delighted in bringing as many people into it as she could, and thirty years later, she's *still* organizing fun get-togethers!

PITFALLS

GREEN people tend to judge themselves by their own good intentions rather than by what they actually *did*. I call this the it's-the-thought-that-counts mentality. The mother of a GREEN student lamented that when her son finished his homework, it was so illegible that she made him redo it. He couldn't understand why he had to do it again after he'd already done it once. After all, he *wanted* to do a good job, he *meant* to do a good job, and he really *tried* to do a good job. The fact that his actual output was completely illegible didn't seem to register. GREEN needs to learn that quality work leads to quality results, and there is no shortcut for hard work, no matter how engaging their personality is!

GREEN is such a big picture person that he or she will often miss important details. It is crucial to make sure that GREEN students write *all* the pertinent information for a learning task in *one* place where they can see it.

MOTIVATION and RESISTANCE

GREEN people are motivated by bringing others into their vision. They will always try their best in school because they want to do a good job, and they want to please their coaches and teachers. Resistance manifests most at home with members of the GREEN's family, especially parents. Though GREEN kids are eminently coachable by those outside their family, they feel wounded when they encounter correction or criticism from their inner circle. For this reason, parents of GREEN students should allow the teachers to make technical corrections. The GREEN student will do almost anything to avoid the feeling of parental rejection, manifesting in procrastination or avoiding work altogether. Parents of GREEN students should focus solely on encouraging their children to do the things they can *already* do well, thereby raising their ability, and leave all correcting and fixing to their teachers.

COLOR	Learning Style	Thinking Style	Verbal Expressiveness	Natural Pace	Temporal Orientation	Time/ Space	Time Urgent/ Time Patient	Motivation	Resistance
Green	Kinesthetic	Global	First talker	Fast	Early Action	Space: Psychological	Urgent	Bring everyone on board with their ideas	Procrastination and refusal to work

BLUE

Behavioral Characteristics

- Independent
- Good at almost everything
- Adaptable, flexible
- Non-confrontational
- Diverse interests
- Don't want games, just show them what to do
- Visual learners
- Linear thinkers who then process globally
- Medium fast pace
- Intuitive time awareness
- High standard of personal excellence
- Like to know what's going on/be in the loop but keep their own personal information to themselves
- Ask a lot of "why" questions—they have to know!
- Like peace and safety (not big risk takers)
- Like to make lists and check off tasks as they complete them
- Generous
- Friends with all sorts of different people, good networkers
- Can be very consistent, like routine
- Strong sense of appearance/how they look; they like things that look cool
- Great performers

You can usually spot BLUE right away because:

1. They are always asking questions and

2. They have a strong sense of personal appearance. They don't ever want to look bad: wardrobe-wise and competency-wise. They will most likely look good!

However, BLUE will not ask lots of questions initially in a group and may even seem aloof at first in class. They don't speak first because they need to watch carefully first to see what's going on and what the expectations are. My daughter Mercedes is taking a history class with a really tough professor. She observed for the first month while her classmates kept raising their hands and getting shot down. In week six, Mercedes raised her hand and got praised for her comments. That's BLUE.

It's important for BLUE to feel in control. BLUE craves peace and safety. If an activity or situation seems unsafe and they might fail, they will take control in any way they can.

VISUAL LEARNERS

BLUE is a "watch-and-copy" visual learner who learns best by watching what the teacher is doing and copying it. They catch on very quickly when they have someone demonstrating what to do. Young BLUE students need tasks to be broken down into manageable bits. They don't like to take risks, so if they're unsure whether or not they can execute the skill correctly, they might resist. Breaking the skill down into parts ensures that they will feel safe to try it.

BLUE students do best when they have visual or written examples to copy and compare to their own work. If possible, BLUE students should video lessons or tasks so that they can refer back to them.

LINEAR-GLOBAL THINKERS

BLUE first processes information in a linear fashion, step by step. And BLUE *loves* lists! What could be more linear than a list? Young BLUE students enjoy putting stickers on a chart to keep track of their progress. (This strategy also appeals to BLUE's attraction to things that look cool.) However, after BLUE has processed the information step by step, she is then likely to put it into a big picture context. BLUE sees opportunities that others miss due to their ability to process information globally. Once they have examined information one by one, in the linear phase of their processing, that task or information belongs to them. Once they own it, it ceases to pose a risk and they are then able to use it in a big picture context, allowing them to apply what they have learned in new ways.

MEDIUM FAST PACE

BLUE experiences life at a medium fast past and is also time urgent. They need their work to be finished on time, so much so that they will often finish well in advance of a deadline.

TIME AWARE

BLUE experiences time in an intuitive manner. They internally know *when* to do a given thing to get the best outcome. In the marble analogy, BLUE sees all the marbles and instinctively knows *which* particular marble to play at any given time for the optimum result.

When confronted with deadlines at school, for example, BLUE will usually get the work done ahead of the deadline on *their* schedule. This means that BLUE has an *early action* temporal orientation.

When working with a very young BLUE student, parents should establish a work routine; however, once BLUE gets to be old enough, parents can give the student the task of determining when they will do their work each day. This means that the parent must make themselves available to help BLUE students whether they choose to work before school or after school. One of my BLUE studio mothers has worked out this exact approach with her BLUE daughter to great effect. "She knows she has to practice her guitar every day, and it's up to her to fit it in," she explained. This works because BLUE has a high personal standard of excellence, can be trusted to do their work, and has an internal awareness of timing.

Interestingly, the above BLUE student chooses to practice in the morning. This dovetails with the idea of *early action*, namely getting work done well *before* the deadline so it's not hanging over her later.

When I was the Suzuki violin practice partner for my BLUE daughter, my RED sense of urgency prevented me from even considering such a radical option. Let my daughter decide when to practice? No way! Well, now that she's a young adult, this is exactly how she approaches the violin, allowing her own internal clock to guide her practice routine.

PITFALLS

BLUE can get discouraged and view the world as a "glass half empty." I call it the BLUE wet blanket syndrome. Upon hearing good news, the BLUE wet blanket will say something like, "Well, okay, but . . ." and point out why that news isn't all that great. Instead of joyfully looking at the positive, BLUE can fixate on all the potential problems. To avoid the wet blanket syndrome, BLUE people should find *uplifting* things that make them smile or laugh every day, even if it's something small, and keep a journal. BLUE should also surround themselves with people who have an upbeat attitude. If they surround themselves with negativity, they tend to absorb it and lose their sense of possibility, which manifests in the inability to enter into someone else's joy.

If a BLUE student does not see the benefit in a task, she can easily act out without remorse, failing to understand how her bad attitude can be hurtful to others. Because of their strong sense of independence, BLUE people might resist leadership and can be very critical of poor or struggling leaders, bosses, or supervisors. It takes a lot to impress BLUE! BLUE's strong sense of internal timing can lead to resistance when a parent or teacher asks him to do something, and this can come across as stubbornness. Interdependent tasks with others can be difficult when BLUE students insist on doing things on their own time rather than making more of an effort to coordinate with others.

MOTIVATION and RESISTANCE

BLUE people are motivated by watching, doing, or making things that look cool, and they like to demonstrate their high standards of personal excellence. BLUE people crave peace and safety and are low risk-takers, so they will procrastinate if a task seems too risky. Rather than risk failure, a young BLUE child may act out by engaging in silly talk, spinning around on his seat, or running around the room. A BLUE child would rather get in trouble and bear a consequence that she *knows* will happen than try something new or go somewhere unknown, because that would be too risky. This seems out of character for BLUE, who is usually reserved and well-behaved. When BLUE children act out, they are saying, "I don't feel safe; this activity is way too risky for me." When this happens, break down the activity into smaller, less intimidating, easy-to-accomplish tasks.

COLOR	Learning Style	Thinking Style	Verbal Expressive-ness	Natural Pace	Temporal Orientation	Time/Space	Time Urgent/Time Patient	Motivation	Resistance
Blue	Visual Watch and Copy	Linear-Global	Asks lots of questions but not at first in a group; won't offer information	Me-dium Fast	Early Action	Time: Intui-tive	Urgent	To make things that look cool; to show off their hard work	Acting out, silliness, crying or refusal

INDIGO

Behavioral Characteristics

- Implementers
- Fast-paced; quick decision makers
- Expert organizers
- Value loyalty
- Hate monotony
- Thrive under pressure (and like to put others under pressure too), love beating the clock
- Like to be busy and can handle everything they're doing!
- Linear thinker
- Visual learner (written linear)
- Steady-action work style

- Like rules
- Like charts and lists
- Read all the time—*LOVE* to read
- Use imagination in play
- Respond well to direct commands
- Can take an abstract concept and break it down into concrete steps
- Task oriented
- Need freedom to implement their own strategies
- Skilled at time management
- "Can-do" attitude, not afraid to try new things
- Want to go farther and faster and make whatever they're doing bigger and better
- Independent (disinterested in group activity because they don't need the other people, not realizing that the others need them)
- Quick study—can learn new things fast
- Will be satisfied if the job is *mostly* done. This can mean that technique suffers at the expense of covering a lot of ground quickly.

INDIGO has an active imagination, loves to read, and loves to act out or daydream about characters in favorite books. INDIGO may talk a lot, but not at first when in a group.

INDIGO is usually extremely busy and gifted with excellent organizational skills. They can mobilize people to get the job done, no matter what the task. When given an objective, INDIGO can figure out what to do to make it happen. Not only can INDIGO get the job done, but the result is usually bigger and better than anyone could have imagined.

INDIGO loves to accomplish something and then move on to the next task. They hate monotony and repetition. They need a bigger context or a serious challenge in order to make necessary repetitions of a given task palatable and keep them engaged.

INDIGO children usually like to climb on things such as trees, furniture, or playground equipment. They enjoy strategy games and solving puzzles. One of my INDIGO friends liked to make her own puzzles as a child: she was interested in the concept of Pangaea (the idea that the land mass of the world was once connected), so she cut out all the continents and islands from a world map and then tried to fit the pieces together.

INDIGO cares deeply about rules. Once I had an INDIGO student who would always act out in group guitar class. He was constantly getting in trouble with me, other teachers, other kids, and even other parents. This went on for years until I finally figured out that I needed to make clear and concrete rules. The two rules of group class were:

1. Raise your hand if you have something to say.
2. Only play your instrument if you are asked to play or if the whole group is playing together.

At the beginning of every group we recite The Two Rules, and I enforce the rules by adding a small Starburst candy block to a tower on my music stand for every time the class follows the rules. If there is any illegal talking or playing, a block is removed from the Rules Tower. At the end of the class, if there are as many blocks in the tower as there are students, then everyone receives a reward! If there aren't as many blocks as students, then no one gets a reward that day.

Implementing clear, concrete, and enforceable rules transformed my INDIGO student from being the class disrupter into becoming one of the class leaders. I now sit him near other students who might have trouble with illegal talking and playing, and I have marveled watching him exert his natural leadership skills to help those kids follow the rules.

So, what was the big difference? The rules were not new—I *never* wanted the kids to play out of turn or blurt things out randomly in class—but when these rules were only implied, they were not *real* to INDIGO. Once I made a concrete representation of the class expectations (in the form of the Starburst tower), the rules became real and all the behavior problems disappeared.

An INDIGO student responds best when very clear rules are established beforehand. In a music evaluation, for example, an INDIGO student responds well when I lay out concrete and clear rules in the beginning: "I'm watching for X,Y, and Z when you play this line." Or try using clocks or metronomes to evaluate instead of the teacher's more subjective feedback.

VISUAL LEARNERS

INDIGO is a visual written linear learner. Because they are more time aware than space aware, INDIGO students don't understand a spatial depiction such as a diagram as well as they do a *written* description. INDIGO people *love* to read. They love stories and often imagine themselves as the characters they've read about. This is why presenting new or difficult information as a linear narrative (in pictures and words) is an effective way for INDIGO to absorb a lesson.

LINEAR THINKERS

INDIGO best processes information in a linear manner. They love day planners and charts. They have excellent organizational skills.

MEDIUM FAST PACE

INDIGO picks up new information quickly but does not go at the blazing speed of RED or GREEN.

TIME AWARE

INDIGO kids thrive on pressure and actually enjoy deadlines—they love to beat the clock! Simply give them the objective and a deadline and turn them loose. Since INDIGO kids experience time as a challenge, keep them under time pressure in order to keep them engaged; otherwise, they will lose interest. When you give an INDIGO student an objective, connect it to a deadline: you have *thirty seconds*—how many correct repetitions can you do? When INDIGO beats the clock, next time ask her if she can do more. She will rise to the occasion. The stopwatch is also useful to slow down a sloppy performance. Time the passage and ask INDIGO, "Can you play it twice as slow this time?"

In the marble analogy, INDIGO would want to collect as many marbles as fast as possible and then arrange them into something really magnificent. INDIGO possesses the ability to look at a long-range project and then figure out how to accomplish the goal in a timely manner. When given an assignment, INDIGO will first note the due date. INDIGO people are visual linear learners and love to chart out a schedule and assignments in a day planner where they can see all of their workload assignments, expectations, and due dates. Then they will complete the overall assignment, task by task, in a *steady-action* deadline style.

When working with INDIGO students, be sure to give them plenty of freedom to solve the problems in their own way. In other words, do not micromanage them. Once they understand the objective, they can come up with their own strategy. It's important to realize that INDIGO values time urgency over quality work, so the key to working with INDIGO kids is to help them define their goals so that they don't just try to cover all their assignments as fast as possible. Make sure detailed objectives are written down at the forefront of the INDIGO student's planner.

PITFALLS

INDIGO kids' "bigger, better, father, faster" attitude may result in a loss of quality in their work. INDIGO can easily fall into focusing on the time it takes to do a given project at the expense of the more important underlying goal. Therefore, it is important to make sure INDIGO students review their work objectives before beginning a project. It can also help to set out smaller objectives within a given project, setting each with its own deadline; this works perfectly with INDIGO's steady-action approach and helps them slow down their work.

MOTIVATION and RESISTANCE

INDIGO children are motivated by going bigger, better, farther, and faster and when there's no opportunity to do that, they aren't keen to participate. INDIGO will procrastinate if the project is monotonous and doesn't engage them. INDIGO students have a tendency to melt down when they are micromanaged. Young INDIGO children cry when they feel powerless or frustrated with people.

INDIGO works well with RED because RED will provide a vision and INDIGO will run with it and figure out how to make it happen. Suzuki Guitar Co-Founder Frank Longay and Kim Buller manifested this dynamic beautifully. RED Frank generated all sorts of new ideas, while INDIGO Kim took these ideas and gave them structure by creating manuals, forms, databases, and all the support materials needed to bring Frank's vision of the Longay Conservatory of Guitar to life. When Kim and Frank collaborated to create the first International Suzuki Guitar Festival, bringing together Suzuki students and teachers from all over the world, it was that RED/INDIGO synergy that made it so successful!

Frank Longay (standing) leading the Final Gala Concert of the first ever International Suzuki Guitar Festival in 2008. Photo by Stephan Hoerold, used with permission.

COLOR	Learning Style	Thinking Style	Verbal Expressive-ness	Natural Pace	Temporal Orientation	Time/ Space	Time Urgent/ Time Patient	Motivation	Resistance
Indigo	Visual Written Linear	Linear	Talkative, but not a first talker	Medium Fast	Steady Action	Time: Thrives under pressure	Urgent	To go bigger, better, farther, faster	Melt down, cry

VIOLET

Behavioral Characteristics

- Verbal expressive but not a first talker
- Like to build a complete ecosystem, create a big picture where each component is aligned, in the perfect place
- Spatially oriented
- Circular thinkers
- Look at things from every possible angle, which can result in moving at a slower reaction speed than a more linear person
- Have great imaginations, like to make up their own stories
- May be reluctant to try new things
- Non-competitive

- Complete visual learners, can function in all visual modes
- Highly sensitive, react with their emotions
- Give up if a task gets too hard or if they aren't emotionally supported
- Intuitive
- Resist being re-engineered—they don't want to be "fixed"!
- Drawn to beauty
- Very slow decision makers
- Steady-action temporal orientation
- Don't respond well to direct commands, prefer to be drawn into a larger scenario
- Don't respond well to competitive games—they don't care if they win!
- Don't respond well to linear things such as charts
- Respond well to stories and enjoy sense of discovery
- Love to read
- Can be fantastic performers
- Passion for excellence
- Resist change and adapt to change slowly

VIOLET is dreamy, imaginative, and can appear spacey. VIOLET children are easy to spot. They are the kids who routinely make seemingly random comments in school, at home, and everywhere else. You think you're discussing A, and then the VIOLET blurts out X—something so far removed from the topic that it seems to have come from outer space! To those who misunderstand the dreamy nature of VIOLET, these children can seem like space cadets.

Parents of VIOLET kids spend their days urging and pleading for their son or daughter to *focus,* to no avail. Frustration ensues for everyone. This is, in part, due to VIOLET's circular thinking style and in part because VIOLET is designed to dream and to bring their dreams into reality. Unfortunately the process of dream realization gets thwarted or squashed by everyone else who wants to coerce VIOLET to get with *their* program, to stay on topic, see the world as they see it, and above all to abandon their childish behavior.

I have watched this cycle of frustration play out over and over again during guitar lessons. Time with the instrument devolves into a big power struggle. Much unhappiness ensues for the parent and the child, who wonders why his mom or dad is so unhappy with him. VIOLET defaults to feeling guilty. They don't want to upset their parents. It is easier for them to avoid the offending activity (to quit) than it is to change. VIOLET strongly resists being "fixed" or changed. They have a beautiful vision of how each component in their life should work, and they do not take kindly to someone who wants to interfere with it. VIOLET is the most stubborn of all the *Life Lens* types.

In the process of trying to fit in with their family and at school, VIOLET children become adept at speaking non-VIOLET languages just to survive, but underneath the surface they resent having to change the essence of who they are.

VIOLET people's emotional sensitivity is their great strength and gift, but this sensitivity can also be turned against them when others trample uncaringly over their tender feelings. VIOLET must have emotionally supportive people around to take the time to listen to how they feel about a given issue. When VIOLET's feelings are acknowledged their resistance will diminish. Parents of VIOLET children should become fluent in the language of feelings acknowledgement laid out in Adele Faber and Elaine Mazlish's classic book *How to Talk So Kids Will Listen, And Listen So Kids Will Talk* (1980).

Think of VIOLET as a walking heart. They are motivated by love, beauty, compassion, and kindness. They can be inspired but get discouraged easily when threatened, nagged, or browbeaten. VIOLET people function best when they feel loved and accepted and must feel free to experience the world in their own unique way without fear of being changed or "fixed" by those close to them.

VISUAL LEARNERS

VIOLET people are visual watch-and-copy learners. They need to *see* the task demonstrated to best learn how to do it themselves. They can also function well with written linear and written diagrammatic presentations, which distinguishes them from the other visual learners who have only one best way of learning. VIOLET is the complete visual learner.

CIRCULAR THINKERS

VIOLET processes information in a circular manner. They take all the components into account and then consider the elements from many different angles and perspectives. VIOLET people want to create the big picture with the pieces they have been given, continuously circling back to extract the most amount of value or meaning from each individual component.

To illustrate, picture a person surrounded by a semi-circle of computers all open to different topics. To the outside observer (you), each computer displays completely unrelated topics, but to the VIOLET circular thinker each topic is relevant and connected to the others. Though she might not be able to articulate what that connection is, VIOLET works on one computer for a while and then spins around to work on something utterly different, moving back and forth among the topics on the other computers all day long. At times she can get so caught up in the minute details of what she is working on that she utterly loses sight of the big picture of whatever it was that she was supposed to be doing, but it is important and necessary for her to fully explore each computer's topic.

SLOW PACE

VIOLET experiences life at the slowest pace of all. It takes a lot of time to consider something from every angle before responding.

SPACE AWARE

The VIOLET concept of space is "everything in its place functioning perfectly." VIOLET people crave a complete ecosystem in everything they do, where every component functions beautifully and well. This is not only true for physical space but for emotional space, where everyone is happy and functioning perfectly in his or her place. Creating such quality takes time. VIOLET people do not respond well to nagging; in fact, this can slow them down even more. Give them plenty of time and don't rush them.

VIOLET people release their creativity best when they work in a *steady-action* deadline style.

Often VIOLET needs time to just sit and think about the

task. To a time-aware person, this makes it look like VIOLET is ignoring the task or spacing out. Since they are not *doing* the task, they appear to be inert; however, they cannot just spring into action without having carefully considered all the possible angles and implications of the project. Because VIOLET is very time patient and will always prioritize perfection before meeting a deadline, and also because they need lots of time to mull over and process a project between times they are actually doing the project, it is important for VIOLET to start right away and work continuously so that all will be in place before the deadline.

PITFALLS

VIOLET can be emotionally manipulative. One of my five-year-old VIOLET guitar students arrived at my studio having decided that he didn't want to have his lesson that day. When his mom excused herself to use the restroom, he folded his arms defiantly and said, "I'm not going to play, and you can't make me." I calmly responded, "That's okay. You don't have to play, but you're not going to play on your iPad either. You can just listen to me play through the book." When his mom returned, to her credit, she did not interrupt or ask what was happening. She just sat there. He just sat there. And I played from the end of Suzuki Book 1 toward the beginning. Eleven songs (out of fourteen) into the process, the student picked up his guitar, sat down, and joined me for the last three pieces. His attempt to emotionally manipulate me didn't work, and he decided it was more fun to join in than to just sit and listen. VIOLET can be stubborn! To help them, explain *why* you're asking them to do what you want them to do.

VIOLET people might also blame others when things don't go well for them. "You didn't teach me that part," whined the VIOLET student after she couldn't remember one line in her current guitar piece. Her father kindly pointed out that she had worked on that very line all week long at home and that it wasn't right to blame the teacher or anyone else. The key here is that her dad was gentle and kind even as he disabused the student of her blame shifting. VIOLET children thrive when they have an emotionally supportive person alongside them.

MOTIVATION and RESISTANCE

VIOLET is motivated by creating a perfectly functioning, beautiful whole. They are highly sensitive and react according to their emotions, so positive feedback and recognition of their feelings are paramount. VIOLET students may procrastinate if they feel a task is irrelevant; they must feel that the task is important. VIOLET also might resist if there are too many steps involved. They may just decide not to do the problematic task and simply quit. When frustrated, they may retreat into their own make-believe world. If feeling overwhelmed, VIOLET students might put their heads down, whine, or cry.

COLOR	Learning Style	Thinking Style	Verbal Expressiveness	Natural Pace	Temporal Orientation	Time/ Space	Time Urgent/ Time Patient	Motivation	Resistance
Violet	Complete Visual; Watch and Copy	Circular	Talkative, but not a first talker	Slowest	Steady Action	Space: Beautiful and Functional	Time: Patient	To create a beautiful, complete emotional and spatial ecosystem	Whining, crying, quitting

Life Lens REFERENCE TABLE

	RED	ORANGE	YELLOW	GREEN	BLUE	INDIGO	VIOLET
Learning Style	Kinesthetic	Auditory	Visual Written Diagrammatic	Kinesthetic	Visual Watch and Copy	Visual Written Linear	Complete Visual; Watch and Copy
Thinking Style	Linear	Linear	Global-Linear	Global	Linear-Global	Linear	Circular
Verbal Expressiveness	First talker	Not talkative, will talk in a group only by special request	Will never talk first	First talker	Asks Questions; doesn't offer information unless asked	Talkative	Talkative
Pace	Fastest	Slow	Slower	Fast	Medium Fast	Medium Fast	Slowest
Temporal Orientation	Deadline	Steady	Deadline	Early	Early	Steady	Steady
Time Urgent/ Time Patient	Urgent	Patient	Patient	Urgent	Urgent	Urgent	Patient
Time/Space	Time: internal awareness	Time: monotasker	Space: functional	Space: psychological	Time: intuitive	Time: thrive under pressure	Space: beautiful ecosystem
Motivation	Solving Problems	Helping Others	To find functionality for each part	To bring everyone on board with their ideas	To make something that looks cool, show their hard work	To go bigger, better, farther, faster	To create a complete ecosystem, spatially and emotionally
Resistance	Defensive	Whine, complain, cry	Non-participation	Procrastination, refusal to work	Acting out, silliness, refusal	Melt down, cry	Whine, cry, quit
Other	Visionary; create new things	Follow instructions to a T; trustworthy	Non-judgmental	Cause and effect	Stewardship: taking a skill they have and multiplying it for the greater good	Making functional systems	Alignment and love

Chapter 3: ART IMITATING LIFE

Have you found yourself yet in one of the *Life Lens* types? If not, don't worry. Let's try a different way of looking at how *Life Lens* shapes who we are. Below, I'll examine some famous real-life individuals and favorite characters from television and film. If you don't share my taste in entertainment, that's okay. The characters that interest me don't necessarily matter, but the idea that a person resonates with people and characters who are like them *does* matter. Taking notice of your favorite characters, both fictional and from real life, can provide strong clues to the *Life Lens* types of your children, students, family members, or yourself. If a character or person reminds you of yourself or another person, there's a good chance the similarity is *Life Lens* related.

RED CHARACTERS

BATMAN

In Batman we have an ideologically driven action hero devoted to justice. This is so RED. A great injustice is done to Bruce Wayne as a boy when he witnesses the murder of his parents, and he responds by swearing revenge on all criminals. Bruce overcomes his fears and trains himself to become Batman. Batman has a lot of cool gadgets, displaying RED's love of technology! Batman solves all sorts of puzzles as he foils criminals and beats them up, proving his kinesthetic and very physical REDness.

GIMLI

Gimli the dwarf from *The Lord of the Rings* books and movies is so obviously RED, because he offers a running commentary throughout the *entire* epic quest! You always know exactly what Gimli's opinion is about everything. Gimli is a fierce warrior for good who never backs down, even when outnumbered. He welcomes the challenge! Unceasingly competitive, Gimli keeps track of all the evil orcs he dispatches. Gimli also has to overcome his distrust of Legolas the elf because he is bitter about a perceived wrong that the elves did to the dwarves many years before. When Gimli is brought to a council where he learns that the "ring of power" must be destroyed, he springs into action immediately and tries to break the ring himself by swinging down his trusty axe! RED Gimli couldn't wait for the specific instructions of *how* the ring must be destroyed. This is typical RED—act first and sort out the details later.

STEVE JOBS

I was moved to tears by Ashton Kutcher's portrayal of Apple founder Steve Jobs in the biopic *Jobs*. The movie did not meet with critical or box office success (Wloszczyna 2013), but something about Steve Jobs deeply resonated with me—his REDness! Jobs was a tireless innovator who ended up getting thrown out of his own company because of his unwillingness to compromise his beliefs. Think of all the products that we use every day that didn't exist before Steve Jobs created them, things like the iPod, iPad, iPhone, mobile apps, and the App Store. Steve Jobs was a true visionary who also suffered a number of broken relationships when those around him fell out of agreement with his ideas. In the film, Kutcher nails Steve Jobs's positive and negative RED characteristics, both the RED vision to create something that hasn't existed before, and the RED propensity to rub people the wrong way due to their strong opinions and intransigence.

ORANGE CHARACTERS

HUGO

The title character from the 2011 movie *Hugo* beautifully depicts the ORANGE *Life Lens*. The protagonist, Hugo Cabret, epitomizes the steady-action ORANGE style—he winds clocks in a train station. What could be more steady than that? Hugo also keeps a low profile, living out of sight between the walls of the station. He seems to have a cloak of invisibility as he quietly and competently goes about his business, which is so ORANGE. He experiences joy in fixing things so that they can function, but his real purpose is to help the people around him discover *their* purpose so that they can function. Hugo says, "If you lose your purpose, it's like you are broken" (Scorsese 2011). An ORANGE's greatest fulfillment comes when he helps others, and ORANGE Hugo steadfastly works to help the broken people in his life find their purpose. Hugo relates differently to each of the other characters in the movie. With one he is persistent, with another he keeps a safe distance, with another he talks more, and with another he talks less and shows evidence instead. Although some relationships are more difficult than others, in the end, Hugo's consistent approach wins the day—a great picture of the amazing ORANGE ability to joyfully interact well with everyone!

CAPTAIN AMERICA

Captain America is my favorite example of an ORANGE super-hero. He only wants to help. ORANGE characters do not have their own agenda to take over the world—Captain America is not motivated by revenge or wanting to draw attention to himself. He has a big heart utterly devoid of guile and full of humility.

When he becomes Captain America, his body reflects the excellence of his inner character, and his purpose is to help others.

BOOKER T. WASHINGTON

The famous author, educator, and civil rights leader Booker T. Washington lived to serve others, which means he is ORANGE. He said so himself: "If you want to lift yourself up, lift up someone else." (1900) He also said, "I learned long ago that those who are happiest are those who do the most for others." No statement could be more ORANGE.

YELLOW CHARACTERS

NOAH WEBSTER

In 1807 Noah Webster began compiling an expanded and fully comprehensive dictionary, An American Dictionary of the English Language; it took twenty-eight years to complete. To evaluate the etymology of words, Webster learned twenty-six languages, including Old English (Anglo-Saxon), German, Greek, Latin, Italian, Spanish, French, Hebrew, Arabic, and Sanskrit. Webster hoped to standardize American speech, since Americans in different parts of the country used different languages. They also spelled, pronounced, and used English words differently. Webster personifies the qualities of YELLOW: detail-oriented, slow-paced, methodical, likes lists, needs plenty of time to practice or learn a new thing, neither accepts nor rejects new information immediately but must study ALL of the details from many different angles before moving forward with it, cares deeply about accuracy, likes to delve deeply into a topic, and enjoys factoids.

THE LIBRARIAN's **FLYNN CARSEN**

A few years ago, I saw a trilogy of TV movies called *The Librarian,* starring Noah Wyle. Wyle's character, the librarian Flynn Carsen, solves mysteries and gets out of sticky situations due to all of the knowledge he has amassed. He pulls out just the right information needed to succeed in the moment. Flynn Carsen is a kind of anti-action hero who appears bumbling and ill-suited to face the forces of evil but, due to his brilliance, proves uniquely qualified to protect the world from a variety of threats. *The Librarian* depicts a perfect example of a YELLOW character, one who enjoys learning even seemingly insignificant things because one day that knowledge may come in handy. YELLOW loves to find functionality for the information they've learned. In the following dialogue, Flynn interviews for the job of librarian. Charlene, played by Jane Curtin, grills Flynn to find out why he's qualified to be The Librarian. Flynn gets the job due to his ability to call on his massive knowledge base and apply just the right combination of information to win the day.

> **Charlene**: *What makes you think you could be The Librarian?*
>
> **Flynn Carsen**: *Well, I've read a lot of books.* [laughs]
>
> **Charlene**: *Don't try to be funny. I don't do funny.*
>
> **Flynn Carsen**: *I'm sorry.*
>
> **Charlene**: *[after a pause] What makes you think you could be The Librarian?*
>
> **Flynn Carsen**: *I know the Dewey Decimal System, Library of Congress, research paper orthodoxy, web searching. I can set up an RSS feed . . .*

Charlene: *Everybody knows that. They're librarians. What makes you think you are* The *Librarian?*

Flynn Carsen: *[confused] I know other stuff?*

Charlene: *Mr . . . Flynn Carsen, stop wasting my time. Tell me something you know that nobody else who has walked in here could tell me.*

Flynn Carsen: *[examining her] You have mononucleosis. Your marriage broke up two months ago. You broke your nose when you were four, and you live with three cats. Is that what you had in mind? Swollen parajugular lymph nodes and distended eyelids are clearly mono. It takes three months for an indentation on the ring finger to completely disappear. Yours is two-thirds gone. Your plastic surgeon gave you a terminus paralateral scar, which is given to children under the age of six. And I can clearly see three distinct types of cat hair: a white Himalayan, a tortoiseshell, and an orange-striped tabby.*

Charlene: *[slightly embarrassed] I didn't break my nose until I was five* (Titcher, Roskin, and Peak 2004).

DR. "BONES" BRENNAN

Dr. Temperance Brennan is the "Bones" character from the TV series *Bones* (Hanson 2005). She suffers from that know-it-all persona that many YELLOW types have to learn how to reign in. She's brilliant and really good at her job and sometimes a little too correct about everything. She doesn't tolerate people who aren't as good at their jobs, but she really cares about her friends and co-workers, and her humanity shines through when she interacts with them. This is a great example of YELLOW.

GREEN CHARACTERS

BILL CLINTON

Remember how President Bill Clinton used to take opinion polls about everything? It's because he is GREEN—he cared what others thought and wanted others to like him. He also exemplified GREEN's It's-the-thought-that-counts mentality when he famously proclaimed, "I did not have sex with that woman!" The GREEN mind thinks, "I didn't mean to, I didn't want to; therefore, I didn't do it." More importantly, Clinton exemplifies the GREEN desire for everyone to be in the same psychological space. Clinton stated it himself, "We all do better when we work together. Our differences do matter, but our common humanity matters more" (FDCH E-media 2004).

OPRAH WINFREY

As host and supervising producer of the *The Oprah Winfrey Show,* Oprah Winfrey created an unparalleled connection with people around the world. The very nature of Oprah's work is GREEN— connecting people and bringing them into her psychological space. Oprah has stated her mission in clear terms: "The roles we play in each other's lives are only as powerful as the trust and connection between us—the protection, safety, and caring we are willing to share. Connect. Embrace. Liberate. Love somebody. Just one person. And then spread that to two. And as many as you can. You'll see the difference it makes" (2011). Oprah's gigantic media and philanthropic enterprise is motivated by GREEN's desire for everyone to be psychologically in tune.

Oprah also exemplifies the GREEN quality of fearing

no mistakes and learning by doing: "I will tell you that there have been no failures in my life," Oprah says, "I don't want to sound like some metaphysical queen, but there have been no failures. There have been some tremendous lessons." No mistake is seen as a failure by GREEN, only as a chance to do it again.

RACHAEL RAY

The celebrity cook and author for the everyday American household is another good example of a successful GREEN with a strong work ethic. Rachael says, "Not everybody is interested in what I'm interested in. You have to have a small ego to write effective, everyday recipes. You can have a big ego and be a great chef, but that's not my job. It's my job to *teach people* and appeal to all different lifestyles, age groups and backgrounds." She also says, "The greatest feeling in life is to make a meal and share it with people." GREEN is the consummate people person. GREEN only wants to bring people together!

Here's Rachael giving advice about cooking at home: "So you can't have dinner until around 9 p.m. or 10 p.m. If that's what it is, that's what it is. You can't have it all without sacrificing quite a bit. You can't be too rigid with things like what time you'll have dinner or when you'll take vacation." Rachael advises people to be more flexible, to relax and have fun, to keep the big picture in mind instead of sweating the details. These are all qualities of GREEN. They can do many things simultaneously, the big picture is the most important to them, and they love to have fun!

BLUE CHARACTERS

RAY KROC

Ray Kroc exemplifies the linear-global thinking style of BLUE. He got his start when he bought the McDonald brothers' hamburger stand (demonstrating BLUE's inherent sense of timing). With one small hamburger stand, he learned step by step about the hamburger business (linear processing). Then, when he felt comfortable enough, he bought another hamburger stand and had the idea to make the menu the same. After he became an expert on the inner workings of a hamburger restaurant, Kroc went global (first in his thinking, and then literally global). He essentially created a whole new genre of restaurant—"fast food" (2009). McDonald's provides easy access to food that you know will be consistent. This "knowing-what-you're-getting" factor also appeals to low-risk BLUE. If they are in a strange city or airport, the lowest risk is to go to a place where they know what the food will be like versus having to try something unknown (Burk 2000).

BILL GATES

Bill Gates's professional life demonstrates the linear-global thinking style of BLUE. Gates wrote computer code for many years (linear processing) and then had the global idea to write code that *anyone* could use. Microsoft software made computing accessible to everyone. You don't have to be a programmer to use it. BLUE Gates is very private about his personal life but is not shy about getting involved in world affairs. Famously curious, inquisitive, time intuitive, and always demanding a high standard of personal excellence, Gates is classically BLUE.

Even though he is one of the the wealthiest people in the world and has been very successful in his business and his foundation, Gates doesn't show his BLUE generosity before studying, asking lots of questions, and being sure about a project's worth before he donates to it or gets involved in it. This is because of his BLUE affinity for peace and safety (Burk 2000).

MAJOR CRIMES' SHARON RAYDOR

I confess to being something of a TV crime drama junkie. (Chalk it up to my RED interest in problem-solving.) I've been captivated by the TNT series *Major Crimes*, the spinoff to *The Closer*, because of my admiration for BLUE protagonist Captain Sharon Raydor, played by Mary McDonnell (Duff, Shephard, Belanoff, and Wallace 2012). Captain Raydor maintains a calm and quiet demeanor. She works within the context of the rules but always seems to find ways to proceed that no one else has considered—a wonderful quality of BLUE. Raydor has serious networking skills and a high level of personal excellence that complement her intuitive sense of timing. Viewers will even catch a glimpse of BLUE's ability to nurture others through Raydor's relationship with a witness she takes into her home (Geter 2012).

INDIGO CHARACTERS

VERA WANG

Vera Wang said, "Although in skating you compete with other people, anyone who achieves a certain level of success is first and foremost competing against themselves. And for me the idea that I could always do better, learn more, learn faster, is something that came from skating. But I carried that with me for the rest of my life" (Becker 2007). The idea that Wang could always do better, learn more, learn faster is classic INDIGO. INDIGO's competitive nature lends itself well to sports. It was Wang's father (who I believe was BLUE because he saw an opportunity that no one else had seen before) who suggested that she start a custom wedding gown business, and this business has certainly gotten bigger and gone farther and faster than most. Wang's bridal gown company has grown to include clothing, cosmetics, accessories, and jewelry. The company made over a billion dollars in 2013 and has locations in twenty countries (Fitzpatrick 2013).

NCIS: LOS ANGELES' *HETTY LANGE*

Once again in the TV crime genre, I turn to the CBS series *NCIS: Los Angeles* (Brennan 2009) for another INDIGO example: Henrietta "Hetty" Lange, Operations Manager of the Naval Criminal Investigative Service's Office of Special Projects in Los Angeles. We know INDIGO people like to do more, go bigger, better, farther, and faster than their peers. Usually you can tell an INDIGO by finding the busiest person who is doing more than anyone else and can handle everything that she's doing. The *NCIS: Los Angeles* Database on wikia.com lists Hetty's accomplishments (Brennan 2011):

> According to Hetty's NCIS personnel file, Hetty:
> - is fluent in Russian, German, Mandarin, Spanish, Czech, Romanian, Hebrew, Arabic, Hungarian, and Pashto;
> - is skilled in Hapkido, Wushu, and Eskrima;
> - earned a Master of Fine Arts degree from the Sorbonne;

- is a graduate of the Ecole de la Chambre Syndicale de la Couture Parisienne;
- attended the Defense Language Institute;
- won a bronze medal competing in the small-bore rifle event at the 1964 Summer Olympics held in Tokyo, Japan (note that in real life this was not a shooting event at the 1964 Summer Olympics);
- is a recipient of the Defense Intelligence Agency Award of Merit, and a CIA Intelligence Star;
- is a member of the Order of Orange Nassau;
- had a prior career in motion picture and stage costuming;
- is a published novelist;
- is a pilot;
- holds the women's senior division record for the ascent of K2; and was born on February 29, 1948.

INDIGO people thrive when they receive an objective and are left to figure out how to accomplish that objective. This is precisely the position in which we find Hetty week after week on *NCIS: LA*. She receives word about some nefarious plot and has to deploy her team to diffuse the situation in a timely manner. Classic INDIGO!

INGVAR KAMPRAD
The founder of IKEA is the quintessential INDIGO. Turn to the Appendix: THE IKEA TOOL to read more about this amazing businessman and his vision.

IRON MAN's *PEPPER POTTS*
The billionaire tech guru-cum-superhero Tony Stark, known as

Iron Man, and his assistant Pepper Pots are a great example of the dynamite RED/INDIGO relationship. Robert Downey Jr.'s Iron Man manifests many characteristics of RED: focused intently on whatever project he's working on to the exclusion of all else, selfish, opinionated, doesn't play well with others, and doesn't care what others think of him.

Gwyneth Paltrow's Pepper Potts is INDIGO because she can keep up with Stark/Iron Man's fast pace. He gives her broad objectives such as "buy art," and she is able to figure out how to accomplish the objective and acquire and curate an art collection (Arad and Feige 2008). In *Iron Man 2*, Stark makes Pepper CEO of his company and leaves it to her how she will manage the Herculean task (Feige 2010). She actually enjoys all of the challenges Stark/Iron Man gives her, she thrives on being under pressure, and she always rises to the occasion. INDIGO is the only *Life Lens* type who could successfully work for Tony Stark.

VIOLET CHARACTERS

J.R.R. TOLKIEN

Tolkien, the English writer, poet, philologist, and university professor, is best known as the author of the classic books *The Hobbit: or There and Back Again*, *The Lord of the Rings* trilogy, and *The Silmarillion*. In these related works, Tolkien invented the entire fictional history of Middle Earth and the creatures who lived there, including writing languages for them—talk about creating a complete ecosystem! This is nothing but VIOLET.

DOWNTON ABBEY's **LORD GRANTHAM**

I've been hooked on *Downton Abbey* since stumbling onto the infamous episode where Mr. Pamuk dies in Season 1 (Fellowes

2010). I thought the show was going to be a murder mystery, so I kept watching. Once I got over my initial disappointment that it wasn't a period murder mystery series, I realized I could enjoy *Downton Abbey* for the richness of the characters. One of those characters, Robert Crawley, the Earl of Grantham, a.k.a. Lord Grantham (played by Hugh Bonneville), impressed me as a strong example of VIOLET. Lord Grantham loves his wife and family and shows compassion and kindness to his servants, treating them like family too. Maintaining the ecosystem of his royal estate, Downton Abbey, is his life's work. VIOLET Lord Grantham adapts to change slowly, resisting the changes that press in on Downton Abbey during World War I. Lord Grantham doesn't seem to realize that the world that he knows and loves is in flux, demonstrating the very VIOLET characteristic of stubbornness!

MARC CHAGALL

The artist Marc Chagall perfectly illustrates how a VIOLET person who receives solid emotional support can accomplish his high calling of putting his inner vision to work and changing the world for the better.

Chagall's wife, Bella, described him as "a sensitive, somewhat neurotic youth, whose clear-sighted gaze was able to penetrate the veil overlying a warm and familiar everyday life and see strange and wondrous aspects of the reality that surrounded him. He was introverted, dreamy, touchy, and affectionate, with a secret narcissism which made him tend to be a little eccentric in appearance and behavior. Full of fantasy, he experienced the excitements of childhood with such intensity that he remained aware of them throughout his life" (Haftmann

1984). The adjectives Bella used to describe Chagall could well apply to VIOLET in general. Thankfully for us, Chagall met Bella early in his life. She was a safe person who enabled him to look at the world in his own way without fear of being judged. VIOLET must have emotionally supportive people in their lives in order to realize their potential.

Marc Chagall exemplifies a mature VIOLET, who found support first from his mother, then from his wife, and later his companion Virginia McNeil. When Chagall declared his desire to study art, his father disapproved, but his mother encouraged him. "He pestered his mother until she took him to an art school run by a local portraitist . . . Chagall, in his late teens, was the only student who used the vivid color violet" (Harriss 2003).

Working from the heart is how VIOLET functions best. Often they cannot articulate *how* or *why* they know something because the VIOLET motivation comes not from thinking but from feeling. They are the most sensitive *Life Lens* type. Everything for VIOLET people begins and ends with how it makes them feel. Chagall divulged the key for fulfilled VIOLET types when he said, "Only love interests me, and I am only in contact with things that revolve around love. If I create from the heart, nearly everything works; if from the head, almost nothing" (Harriss 2003).

STARBUCKS CEO HOWARD SCHULTZ

VIOLET yearns to make connections in a way that is functional, beautiful, and takes care of people. Howard Schultz's vision for transforming what was then the Starbucks Coffee Tea and Spice Company from a small local bean seller to today's worldwide coffee juggernaut is 100 percent VIOLET. Schultz describes walking into the original Starbucks store for the first time: "I knew I was in a special place. I met the founders of the company and really heard for the first time the story of great coffee." VIOLET needs experiences (or businesses) to exemplify a cohesive whole, to have a story, and Starbucks was fitting the bill.

VIOLET often has a feeling about something but can't articulate how they know it's right. They just know. When Schultz was traveling in Italy, he was struck by the number of coffee bars he encountered. An idea then occurred to him: Starbucks should sell not just coffee *beans* but coffee *drinks*. "I saw something," he says, "not only the romance of coffee, but . . . a sense of community. And the connection that people had to coffee—the place and one another." This romance was not easy to cultivate in America, though, at a time when most Americans didn't know a high-grade coffee bean from a teaspoon of Nescafé instant. But VIOLET Schultz's enthusiasm, stubbornness, and high standard of personal excellence brought his vision to life.

In a 2009 interview with CBS, Schultz said of Starbucks' mission, "We're not in the business of filling bellies; we're in the business of filling souls."

In March 2013, Schultz made headlines and won wide applause after making a statement in support of the legalization of gay marriage. After a shareholder complained that Starbucks had lost sales due to its support for gay marriage, Schultz responded, "Not every decision is an economic decision. *The lens in which we are making that decision is through the lens of our people.* We employ over 200,000 people in this company, and we want to embrace diversity. Of all kinds. If you feel, respectfully, that you can get a higher return than the 38 percent you got last year, it's a free country. You can sell your shares in Starbucks and buy shares in another company." While not every VIOLET CEO will have the same political preferences, Schultz's vision of a company that serves more than one purpose, functioning beautifully for both its employees and its shareholders, and Schultz's stubborn insistence on sticking by his decision, are both very VIOLET ways of functioning.

~~~

Sometimes if you're having difficulty identifying your own behavioral characteristics, you can examine the behavior of your favorite characters. Look at what attracts you to them. For instance, you may have noticed from my character examples, above, that I like *action* movies. That's a clue to my kinesthetic learning style. I also mentioned that I'm a fan of crime dramas. That could appeal for several reasons: I like problem solving, I have a strong sense of justice, and I like fast-paced action. All of these point toward my RED *Life Lens*.

If you pay attention to the TV shows, books, and movies that your friends and family enjoy, you may also find clues about their *Life Lens* types. For example, my BLUE daughter enjoys watching *30 Rock*, *The Office,* and *Parks and Recreation*. My colleague Madeleine *also* likes those same shows. Not surprisingly, Madeleine is also BLUE.

Chapter 4: STRATEGIES for SUCCESS

At this point I hope many of you have had at least one "Aha!" moment in which you are recognizing *Life Lens* in yourself or others. It might take some practice, so don't be discouraged. If you are finding yourself still scratching your head a bit, you may either read on or skip to chapter six, where I supply a few diagnostic tools that can help narrow down a person's color. If you are saying to yourself, Okay, Michele, I get it, I get it—can we move on already? The answer is yes, let's move on to some ways we can help our students by recognizing their *Life Lens.*

APPLICATIONS of *Life Lens*: THE PRINCIPLE OF THE BOOKSHELF

I teach in a room that also serves as the library for the church where our Suzuki program is located. The walls are lined with bookshelves filled with lots of old and dusty books. My VIOLET student George took inspiration from the books and asked if he could pick out one book off the shelves and put it on the table as a reward for each correct repetition of his guitar piece. He ended up building an amazing Victorian-style house during the course of his thirty-minute lesson.

Let's imagine how different *Life Lens* types would work within the same context. I purposely present this somewhat esoteric scenario to illustrate the essential principles of *Life Lens*, NOT so that you can copy the bookshelf activity in your home or classroom but to inspire you to apply the principles in your own way. The point is, if you keep in mind the principles in the bullet points I outlined for each *Life Lens*, it shouldn't matter what props or activities you choose in your lesson or practice times—your time with the student will be productive. The converse is also true: if you do not respect the principles of your children's *Life Lens*, your time will not be productive no matter what activity or props you use. Rather than presenting a menu of prepackaged ideas, I'm providing you with the raw materials. The application of principles takes thought and work on your part, akin to cooking a meal. The principles are the groceries. Here are some examples of using the groceries to cook up some sweet practice times.

RED and GREEN—COMPETITION

RED and GREEN students enjoy competition and games. To add a competitive element to the bookshelf activity, we could place ten books in a pile in the middle of the table. A correctly executed task earns a book to the student's pile, while an unsuccessful task means a book moves to the teacher/parent pile. When the middle pile is exhausted, whoever has the most books gets to set them up as "dominos" and knock them over. This would satisfy the urge to compete, a kinesthetic activity, and the desire to have fun. The important difference between RED and GREEN, which parents and teachers must keep in mind when working on anything with these students, is *awareness of mistakes.* RED students are acutely aware when they have made a mistake—the stream of evaluating good vs. bad, right or wrong flows constantly. RED students are notoriously hard on themselves when they make a mistake. I've often witnessed RED students apologize in the middle of playing a piece for me when something doesn't go perfectly. They don't need you to point out what was done incorrectly, and dwelling on the problems only makes the RED angry and defensive.

GREEN students, on the other hand, tend to judge themselves by their own good intentions rather than by the actual quality of their work. They need help to evaluate their performance; otherwise, they will be satisfied with having completed the task regardless of the result. The mother of a GREEN student recounted her experience with her young son's schoolwork: "It was so sloppy, I made him go back and do it all over again." In the student's mind, he *had* done his homework with the best of intentions and was oblivious to its lack of legibility. Utilize the principle of cause and effect when working with a GREEN. Ask them specific, neutral questions regarding the task: "What happens when your pinky finger is flat on the string? What happens when it is curvy?" or "How does it sound when your finger jumps off the string?" "How does it sound when your finger stays down on the string?" or "What can you do to get your fingers to alternate?" Focus the GREEN student's attention toward the specific components that will achieve the desired result.

ORANGE

ORANGE kids enjoy accumulating stuff—action figures, cards, coins, candy, *anything* as long as they can physically pick it up and group it, one at a time. In the bookshelf activity, an ORANGE student would be happy to just keep adding books to their pile for every repetition or correct task. Using an abstract point system is not a good option for ORANGE. Keeping track of points *and* trying to concentrate on the activity distracts ORANGE in ways that physical object rewards do not. They perform best when they can give undivided attention to the task at hand, master it, and then move on to the next task.

YELLOW

The YELLOW student does not accept or reject new information immediately. They need time to examine and process the information thoroughly from every angle before they make it their own. They do not like to have a lot of new information thrown at them. Because they like to go in depth on a given subject, I might give them a technique and ask them to come up with other places where they could use that technique in pieces that they already know.

In our bookshelf game, I would choose some books in advance and lay them face down on the table. YELLOW students like to get the big picture, so this capitalizes on their motivation to see all the books. For every correct work task or repetition they would get to turn over a book to see its cover. YELLOW would probably want to leaf through the book as well before returning to the task at hand.

BLUE

Getting old books off of a shelf probably would not appeal to the BLUE student in a lesson setting. They would likely be happy just doing the work without having a game involved. Games can annoy BLUE kids. They may say something like, "Okay, just show me how to do it," and then they'd quickly catch on and do whatever you showed them. However, BLUE students do like routine, so for a bookshelf activity, I might take a longer term approach by having the student keep track of their consecutive days of practice and then use the books on the shelf to mark the days each week when I see them for their lesson. After the first week we'd put a bookmark by the seventh book on the first row and see how far we could get over the course of the semester. BLUE students like to be rewarded for their work periodically. They don't necessarily need a reward every week but do want recognition for reaching milestones.

Some authors decry the use of rewards for children practicing their instruments or doing schoolwork. Although rewards might not be a great idea for some kids, they are *essential* to keep a BLUE student motivated. Rewards could be going somewhere special, doing something special, or getting something special. The key word here is *special*. BLUE kids like to have their achievements acknowledged and celebrated with something good. Please do not make the mistake that my BLUE daughter's violin teacher made. She initiated a 100-Day Practice Challenge with the promise of a prize for those who completed the challenge. My daughter enthusiastically finished her 100th day of consecutive practice, but the joy of her accomplishment quickly turned to anger and disappointment when her teacher presented her with her reward: a 1,000-Day Practice Chart. Failure to recognize BLUE students for their excellent work will sabotage your relationship with them and severely hamper their desire to continue to do good work for you. Contrast my daughter's experience with my BLUE student Shiloh. Shiloh has happily completed over 800 days of consecutive practice toward her stated goal of 1,000 days. Her parents have escalated the "specialness" of the rewards as her milestones increase. In the beginning they gave her things like pancake breakfasts and special dinners at her favorite restaurant. The next phase of rewards included trips: to the day spa, to a professional baseball game, to Washington DC. For her 800th day they took her to a recording studio to record a CD of her pieces. They are currently brainstorming what the big prize will be for day 1,000.

INDIGO

The bookshelf activity takes on a different configuration when working with an INDIGO student. INDIGO loves a challenge and possesses the inherent will and determination to rise to the occasion. They are expert organizers and thrive on making things run more efficiently. With such a student I may clear off a bunch of bookshelves, creating a gigantic heap of books in the middle of the table. For every correct repetition the INDIGO would be able to take a book off the table and start to organize it. I say start to organize it because I give them the freedom to operate in whatever manner they see fit. How they go about completing the task is up to them. Do not micromanage an INDIGO. Give them the objective: organize the pile of books on the table. Give them the basic rules: you get to take a book off the table after every correct repetition determined by me (the teacher). Give them the time frame: we have thirty minutes. How many books can you get back onto the shelves? This activity viewed through the lens of any other type of student would not be a fun challenge but rather a discouraging drudgery. Thirty minutes to organize a total mess? Where's the fun in that? INDIGO, however, works best under pressure, and they are expert multitaskers. Their heart cry is, "Challenge me!" They want to go bigger, farther, and faster in everything they do. INDIGO adults are easy to identify—just look for people who are extraordinarily busy and are still able to efficiently manage all of their activities.

PARENTS and *Life Lens*

A parent or teacher's *Life Lens* will inevitably influence the way they interact with their children or students in a learning setting. It can be very helpful to develop an awareness of your own expectations and general outlook and ways your *Life Lens* might work with or against other *Life Lens* types in a particular learning-teaching relationship. I will be describing parents in scenarios with their children practicing guitar, but you can apply the behavioral principles to any context.

RED PARENTS

RED parents typically want to accomplish *their* agenda when working at home with their kids and can be quite hard on them as they drive them to complete the task within RED's given time frame, all the while evaluating whether what their kid is doing is right/wrong. RED people are very hard on *themselves*—that's normal for them. Consequently, RED parents don't realize how much pressure they can put on their kids, especially if the child does not share their sense of time urgency.

I've seen the dynamic play out in lessons where the student is completely unaware of time urgency and the RED parent intervenes by saying things like, "You're wasting your time!" or, "Come on, let's focus!" or, worse yet, issues a threat: "Pay attention or we're leaving." In these scenarios, most of the time I'm not worried by the child's behavior and might have been able to direct the lesson in a positive and productive manner, had I not been interrupted. The RED parent, however, sees the situation in a more black-and-white fashion:

- We are at an expensive lesson
- We have thirty minutes to learn something
- Johnny isn't learning at the moment
- This is bad
- I must intervene
- I will threaten Johnny

Not only has the parent interrupted the flow of the lesson, but now Johnny feels worried that he has somehow done something wrong and he's in trouble. This makes it even more difficult to get him up and running and back on track in his lesson. The RED parent just injected fear and negativity into Johnny's experience with his instrument. This is precisely the type of toxic misunderstanding that can be avoided if the RED parent understands his *Life Lens* and the *Life Lens* of his child and makes the conscious effort to subordinate his "normal" driven approach in favor of entering into the child's style.

ORANGE PARENTS

Because ORANGE has the ability to synchronize well with *all* different *Life Lens* types, ORANGE parents do not usually experience difficulty working with either their mono- or multitasking children. I greatly admire the ORANGE parent's ability to create an atmosphere conducive to learning for each child despite their *Life Lens* differences. Generally, these parents are able to seamlessly customize lesson objectives for each child.

However, if the child is GREEN, ORANGE parents need to be careful and focus only on positive comments. ORANGE wants so badly to help others and will want to point out ways to improve, but GREEN kids don't want help from you! They perceive these corrections as personal criticism, and the dynamic will end up driving a wedge in the relationship and preventing progress. Remember to only provide feedback on the aspects of work that the GREEN child is doing well. Leave it to the teacher to provide corrections.

YELLOW PARENTS

The non-judgmental nature of YELLOW is a tremendous asset in a parent practicing music or doing homework with their children. A YELLOW parent doesn't put the child on the defensive by pointing out everything that's wrong but instead comes alongside the child to help her make improvements. YELLOW most often presents information in such a way that the child will see that what they're doing isn't working and decide to make the correction themselves. It's both the strength and the weakness of YELLOW parents that they will give all the reasons to do the right thing and then rely on the child to make the correct decision rather than impose their will on the child. It's a strength when the child does the right thing, and a weakness when they don't. If the child happens to be one of the stronger-willed *Life Lens* types, such as RED, this relaxed approach will not work! The YELLOW parents need to arm themselves with activities that motivate their specific children so that they will do their assigned tasks.

YELLOW parents do best when they create a checklist of things to practice with their child. A checklist will help both the parent and the child make sure they haven't missed anything and will also give them a feeling of accomplishment when they have checked off every task.

YELLOW parents like to have functional space, so *everything* they need must be at their fingertips to do the given task (to the uninitiated this may look like clutter!) This can present some low-grade tension if the YELLOW parent is working with a *Life Lens* type who craves a cleaner work area, such as VIOLET or BLUE, who not only want the space to function well but also want the space to look nice.

YELLOW parents do not like to rush; therefore, they should allow themselves plenty of time to practice with their children. They should avoid trying to squeeze work in at the last minute.

GREEN PARENTS

It's most important for GREEN parents to get on the same page with their child's teacher early on and to buy into the teacher's objectives. Otherwise, the GREEN parent may risk sabotaging, however unwittingly, her child's instruction. This is because GREEN parents can miss important details while they are looking at the "big picture" and need specific tasks to stay focused. It's so important to GREEN parents that their children be happy in their work that they may be susceptible to letting their children procrastinate or move the focus away from the task at hand.

BLUE PARENTS

The best tool for BLUE parents is a video camera at a lesson. Regardless of the *Life Lens* type of the student, the parent also needs to understand and feel comfortable with the lesson material. Video recording the salient moments of the lesson will ensure that the BLUE parent has an example to watch and copy. BLUE people want to remain in their comfort zone, and having a video enables them to revisit the lesson again and again as needed.

Because BLUE has low risk tolerance and wants to feel confident, BLUE parents might not be willing to change their approach and try new ideas because they already have a system with which they feel comfortable. It might help to practice new approaches in private to gain a certain comfort level before implementing a new approach, just as a BLUE student would prefer to do.

INDIGO PARENTS

INDIGO parents should be aware that other *Life Lens* types do not share their love of being under pressure. INDIGO and ORANGE work well together, perhaps because INDIGO has a clear idea of what to do and ORANGE works well when they are told what to do. Also, INDIGO and ORANGE share the *steady-action* work style. INDIGO parents must take care not to put their ORANGE child under time pressure or give them more than one task to complete at a time. The INDIGO parent must subordinate her inherent strengths to best help her ORANGE child realize his potential.

VIOLET PARENTS

Since VIOLET gets along well with all *Life Lens* types, VIOLET parents don't typically have trouble synchronizing with different types of children. They are usually patient and kind. VIOLET parents are all about the complete ecosystem, so they welcome opportunities to expand their responsibilities within an organization and are likely to get involved in meetings and committees. They have a high standard of excellence and want to do a thorough job. However, VIOLET parents can be needy and ask for help with things that they could and should do for themselves. They don't like sudden changes in plans or schedules, so they require a lot of advance notice when changes must happen. When the going gets tough, they're liable to give up unless they get lots of emotional support.

Life Lens DO's and DON'Ts

Here are some practical examples and advice that will give you an idea how the principles of *Life Lens* can inform your teaching and parenting.

RED DEADLINE

RED time sensitivity presents some real banana peels to avoid for both RED students and RED parents. In the case of a RED student, establish a regular, daily practice or homework time; otherwise, the RED child will likely postpone their work until it gets too close to the due date. RED always thinks that they can do it by the deadline! They love to rise to the occasion. They love a challenge! Many topics of study (especially music) unfortunately do not lend themselves well to RED's *deadline-action* approach. Successful music or other study requires daily practice. Parents of RED children must incorporate work and practice time into their daily routine, like brushing their teeth. The sooner the better for establishing a routine, keeping that marble toward the front end of the priority tube.

Since RED is goal-oriented, dividing work or practice time

into smaller goals will help. Practice then becomes an enjoyable process of solving problems and achieving daily goals.

Once the routine is set up, the challenge becomes keeping the RED student fully engaged. RED is always thinking, constantly noticing and evaluating whether things are good or bad, right or wrong. This can sabotage RED students' performance since they tend to fixate on a mistake. To gain control of RED's runaway brain, give the student a kinesthetic activity to do while she is working. If the student is practicing an instrument, have her quietly hum or sing along with what she's playing. This gives the student's brain something constructive to do rather than engaging in a nonstop judgmental dialogue over a wrong note or a bad tone. She will enjoy practice a lot more without undergoing a self-inflicted mental beating over everything that's not right.

Because of their hard-wired awareness of right and wrong, coupled with their craving to be right, RED students get defensive if their parent points out their mistakes. They already know what's wrong! Even the most gentle comment can feel like criticism to RED and make the RED student want to avoid her work. Use a non-judgmental prop, such as a toy or puppet, to deliver suggestions to RED. This may seem silly, but it works! Encourage RED students by focusing on what they are doing well and ask them to engage in their own problem solving when something didn't go so well. RED enjoys problem solving, competing, and winning.

RED UNDER PRESSURE
My guitar student Hudson was playing a halting version of his piece, interjecting "sorry" after every mistake. (Remember: RED

is always aware of mistakes.) He kept cutting off the same note while in the process of shifting from one position to another, creating a choppy effect. I appealed to his competitive RED nature to address the issue: "We're going to play a game, and I'm pretty sure I'm going to win!" I said, "You're going to play that same passage again; only this time you're going to do one push-up for every *E* note you cut off. I will do one push-up for every *E* that rings throughout the shift." Hudson's eyes lit up. Game on!

He then proceeded to get three *E*'s to ring while only cutting off one. We both got on the floor and did our push-ups. The next time through the passage he nailed all four shifts and was delighted, as I then had to do four more push-ups. "Wow. I thought for sure I would win after I heard you play the first time," I lamented. "What was the difference? How come you couldn't do it five minutes ago and now you can?" Without hesitation, and with a big smile on his face, Hudson exclaimed, "I like being under pressure!" So true. Whereas most other colors crumble, RED thrives under pressure.

GREEN PROCRASTINATION

GREEN students require parents to pay close attention to the Inner Circle/Outer Circle dynamic. Because they are motivated when those closest to them are working together with them, they do *not* receive criticism well from those close to them, the "Inner Circle." They can, however, receive correction from an "Outer Circle" person like a teacher or coach. GREEN students are eager to please and will always try their best, and attempts by a parent to correct or "fix" their work will wound them deeply. No matter how gentle or well-intentioned the correction is delivered, GREEN kids perceive it as a personal rejection when it comes from someone they love. It feels to them as if *they* are unacceptable, and they want to avoid that feeling. When faced with perceived rejection, GREEN will either push back, procrastinate, or flat-out refuse to do their work. It's just too emotionally risky. For this reason, parents of GREEN children should leave all the fixing and correction to the teacher and focus work or practice time at home on praising the skills that GREEN does well.

The mother of one of my GREEN guitar students once lamented, "We fight over the correct notes and technique. He will insist he is doing something correctly and will not bend even if the error is glaring. There is nothing he hates more than for both his brother and I to tell him a note is incorrect. I've tried responding in all sorts of ways, e.g., not labeling it as a 'mistake' or 'wrong,' and he totally sees through it." The student, not surprisingly, often resisted when it came to guitar practice. The key to turning this situation around lies in tying into the GREEN motivation of bringing people together. Once I shared the idea of avoiding all "fixing" and correcting during practice with the mother, practice time improved.

You might be wondering, "How can we work together if I'm not allowed to make any corrections?" Parents can instead:

- Focus on what the GREEN student is doing well and ask him to repeat it. The secret to developing fine ability is to raise the level of the things you can already do. You can't develop ability by doing things that you are not yet able to do!
- Focus the GREEN student on cause and effect by asking him, "What happens when your elbow is like

this? What happens when your elbow is like *that?* What do you think you could do to make your elbow like *that?*" This approach puts you on *their* side, supporting them and helping them to figure out the problem—quite different from them feeling rejected!

KINESTHETIC RED and GREEN—CROSSING THE MIDLINE

One concept I have incorporated into my teaching of kinesthetic learners is also used by occupational therapists and practitioners of neurokinesiology. I ask my students to practice focused tasks while "crossing the midline," moving one hand, foot, or eye into the space of the other hand, foot, or eye (Seigneur 2013). Neurokinesiologist Jean Blaydes Madigan (2009) has shown that facility with crossing the midline enhances brain activity in both hemispheres and assists with skills such as reading, writing, and coordinating the body.

For learning guitar, RED and GREEN students have great success after practicing left-hand fingerings on the back of their right forearm, like my student Nayan below.

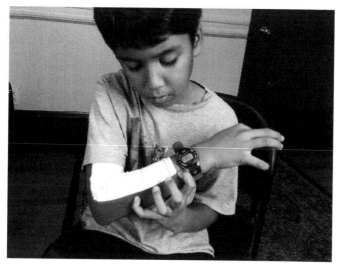

Isolating the correct choreography of the fingers on the oppo-site arm gives the kinesthetic learner a chance to have many correct trials with the benefit of feeling the repetitions in their body. I also have them rehearse right-hand fingerings on their left cheek, as Ryan is doing in the picture below.

It's important for kinesthetic learners of guitar to experience lots of repetitions practicing with their hands separately before attempting to put both hands together on the instrument. Likewise, kinesthetic learners doing any activity will benefit from physical repetitions. Why the "crossing the midline" technique works is a question for brain researchers, but I have seen that simultaneously looking at material and saying it out loud (don't forget that RED and GREEN love to move their mouths as well!) then separately rehearsing fingerings on the opposite sides of the body really helps to efficiently ziplock the information into the kinesthetic learner.

GREEN CAUSE AND EFFECT

One of my studio parents experienced a major breakthrough by utilizing the principle of cause and effect with her GREEN son. My *Life Lens* is RED, and I love to solve problems; however, the key to helping my GREEN student get the proper left-hand shape and keep it while playing his guitar eluded me. My ideas and explanations were not achieving long-lasting results, and we kept revisiting this issue in lessons over the course of years. Ugh.

As the ideas for this book started to come together, I gave my studio parents, including this GREEN student's mother, copies of the *Life Lens* bullet points for their kids. Shortly thereafter, she and her son announced that they had a big surprise for me. He then played his piece with *beautiful* left-hand technique—it was as if a miracle had occurred! The mom told me that she was so happy that she actually cried! What was the secret? The mother simply told the son, "If you move your left elbow in, your hand will rotate into the right position" (cause and effect). The son could hear and receive this message, and what we had been unable to achieve in years was accomplished in one home practice because of the right application of principle.

ORANGE ACCUMULATION

Four-year-old Daniel and his dad had been struggling at guitar time. Daniel whined, procrastinated, cried, and sometimes flat refused to play when it was time to practice. Once I determined that Daniel was ORANGE, I shared the principle of accumulation with his father. At their next home practice, Daniel's dad gave him an empty plastic baggie. For each successful repetition, Daniel got to put a piece of popcorn into his baggie. Using the principle of accumulation, Daniel kept playing and playing, earning another piece of popcorn, and then another, and another, and another. He happily kept right on playing and accumulating popcorn until he filled up his baggie. What a different atmosphere! Guitar became fun again for both Daniel and his dad, thanks to using the right principle.

STICKY FLAG STRATEGY for VISUAL LEARNERS

I've found that using sticky flags works well with my visual learners, especially BLUE and YELLOW. For instance, if I want to position a student's foot properly onto the floor, I simply place a sticky flag on their foot and another on the floor where I'd like the foot to be. If I would like the student to pay attention to the position of their right arm or wrist, I just put a sticky flag on the desired location.

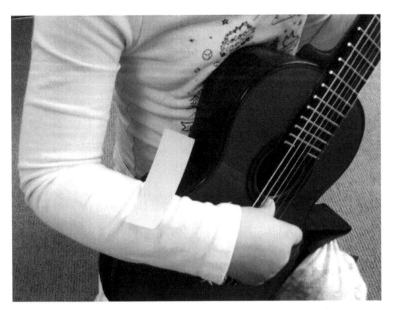

The student now has a visual cue. This strategy also works well in group class settings when I know which kids are visual learners because all I have to do is look around the room, identify technical issues, and then apply sticky flags to the trouble spots for each student.

The sticky flag strategy proves equally useful on practice spots in the music. Rather than having to get an annoying verbal reminder, the visual learner can see exactly what they have to do by glancing at the page. BLUE enjoys lists. Having a page marked with transparent fluorescent sticky flags is akin to having a "to do" list right on the music. At the next lesson, if the spot has been mastered, BLUE gets to remove the sticky flag. Ah! Completing a task gives BLUE a feeling of satisfaction.

Use sticky flags on the body sparingly, especially with YELLOW and VIOLET. Only use them to draw attention to one thing at a time, otherwise they can become a distraction. VIOLET in particular distracts easily.

BLUE RISK AVERSION

BLUE will resist any task or situation that is perceived as too risky. When a BLUE student doesn't want to do something, he might stonewall until you capitulate to what he wants. If a BLUE child thinks you're trying to fix what's wrong with him, he may become even more elusive. The strategy is:

1. Completely take all pressure off
2. Break down skills into manageable bits, reducing or eliminating risk altogether
3. Use lists. Tell them if you do x, y, z you will be able to succeed at _____. Make checklists as a visual representation of progress.
4. Reward periodically for their excellent work. The reward doesn't need to be a daily thing, but every once in a while give them something that they want. Let them pick it.

SHOW NOT TELL to BLUE and VIOLET

Emmy loves the guitar. In spite of this, she and her mother routinely had knock-down, drag-out fights over practicing. Her mom repeatedly told me that she was ready to give up the long-term benefits of studying music because she couldn't handle the day-to-day battles over practicing. Constantly butting heads with each other reveals a lack of understanding of *Life Lens*. The mom cajoled, insisted, bribed, demanded, and threatened, resulting in more frustration for both of them. These tactics never produce lasting results and only plant the seeds of long-term anger and bitterness. The welcome change came when I realized that as a BLUE *Life Lens* type, Emmy is a visual learner. I suggested that instead of talking, her mom should just sit next to Emmy and play along with her. If Emmy got stuck, she could just glance over at her mom's hands to see the correct fingering.

Eliminating talking during home practice immediately made for happier and more productive time together.

When teaching VIOLET, you should also show more and talk less! In a music lesson, for example, you might play the game "My Turn/Your Turn," where you just take turns playing a measure apiece as you make it through a piece. Or you could play a measure or two and then have them copy you. Motivate VIOLET students by allowing them to slowly create their own ecosystem, or story, by using their imaginations. They could use randomly selected photos, sticky flags that you draw on (hat, coat, pants, socks, shoes to make an outfit), a race course, map, or Melissa and Doug Reusable Stickers such as the ones in the photo. In the photo, this student has earned a card with a background scene on it and has placed the reusable stickers that she earned into the scene.

CREATIVE MOTIVATION

Understanding what motivates your children will enable you to hone in on the types of things that *they* enjoy, which are not necessarily going to be the same things that *you* enjoy. The first step toward understanding your child's motivation is to start noticing what they like to do. Observing your child's behavior is also the first step toward understanding their *Life Lens*. For example, my daughter used to love to dress and re-dress her Barbie dolls, creating one "look" after the next. Barbie kept my daughter occupied for hours, and although I personally never liked Barbie, I could see that playing with these dolls held high interest for my daughter. Placing my disdain for Barbie on the back burner, I initiated a new component to violin practice: naked Barbies and a big bucket of clothes. "Oh no! Barbie is naked!" I said. "Every ten practice repetitions will earn one item of clothing to put on Barbie." Far from procrastinating, my daughter now *wanted* to practice her violin and loved getting Barbie beautifully outfitted one item at a time. When the first Barbie was completely dressed and accessorized, she asked, "Can we dress another Barbie?"

I did not know about *Life Lens* types at the time my daughter began studying the violin. Had I realized that my daughter was BLUE it would have made perfect sense to tap into the BLUE affinity to look good. Whether male or female, BLUE always looks good. They have an acute awareness of how they present themselves at all times. Dressing up Barbies ties into that component of the BLUE *Life Lens*.

———————————

Another creative motivation that works especially well for VIOLET is to incorporate the learning task (i.e., guitar) into a bigger scenario. For younger kids, the benefits of learning a particular subject or skill can be lost on them, so they need some other good reason to be doing the task we are setting for them. The trick is to engage the child's interest in such a way that requires her to return to the task again and again. The best way I have found to do this is with a stack of interesting pictures. After every correct repetition the VIOLET child gets to pick a picture and tell you *one* thing about it.

Here's an example: Ask the child, "What's going on in this picture?" (Any picture will do, but see the picture below for an example.) She tells you about it for about thirty seconds to one minute. In order to see the next picture and advance the story, she has to repeat or do another task.

This strategy provides fun for the VIOLET child as well as giving her a chance to exercise her creativity, but within manageable boundaries. Since she enjoys it, she will keep playing to keep the story going and will then want to make another story, and another. The principle that makes the picture game so effective is the principle of circular thinking. VIOLET enjoys taking seemingly disparate elements and weaving them into a connected whole, because this is precisely how she processes information! It is familiar and normal to her.

It may seem like a lot of extra work, and it is, but

I assure you this kind of creative engagement is *not* a waste of valuable time. On the contrary you will accomplish more and have much less conflict in this manner, because you will be working cooperatively with the child's thinking style, precisely what Dr. Suzuki called, "coming down to the child's level of ability and coming up to their sense of awe and wonder about the world."

INDIGO Bigger, Better, Farther, Faster

The desire to go bigger, better, farther, and faster proves problematic if an INDIGO student has decided that conquering her entire musical repertoire is her goal, namely *what* piece she is playing versus how *well* she is playing. Quantity should never outweigh quality! I've encountered several of these students at workshops and institutes through the years. Recently, a father who had been observing my morning master classes approached me at the break. "You're going to have a lesson with my son this afternoon," he warned. "He doesn't like to play any review pieces . . . ever. I'm looking forward to seeing what, if anything, you can do with him." Sure enough, the boy played an incredibly sloppy *Waltz* by Bartolome Calatayud at his lesson. In previous lessons I had been using one or two Starburst candies placed strategically on students' arms to help them focus attention on the desired playing technique. I knew the boy had seen those lessons, so recognizing his need to go bigger, better, farther, faster and to really be challenged, I pulled an entire package of Starburst candy from my bag. "Here it is . . . the mother lode of Starbursts," I said. "One of us is going to end up with all of them." I ripped open the package and put all of the candies on the table. INDIGO rises to the challenge, and true to form this boy applied all of his INDIGO determination toward winning every last Starburst candy by moving methodically through the piece and perfecting, one phrase at a time, every single phrase in his *Waltz*. Rather than focusing on covering more and more repertoire, I simply had to refocus the student toward the goal of making each phrase of his piece work efficiently on its own—which is an inherent strength of INDIGO.

VIOLET—ON GUILT AND BLAME

VIOLET'S default position when something goes wrong is to blame herself and feel guilty. Teachers and parents need to recognize this and realize that the next step is to do whatever it takes to avoid adding more guilt and making the situation worse. Helping VIOLET can be an emotional land mine that will cripple your parent-child or teacher-student relationship if it is not handled skillfully—and by skillfully I'm thinking of Jeremy Renner's bomb technician character diffusing all manner of seen and unseen explosives in the movie *The Hurt Locker*. This requires loads of skill and awareness to avoid blowing up your relationship with condemnation.

Let me give an example to illustrate. During Belle's guitar lesson, her teacher James is working with her on some technical point. VIOLET Belle is trying her best, but she processes new information s-l-o-w-l-y. James understands this and is satisfied with Belle's effort. To Belle's mom, however, it appears that Belle is off task, and she wonders why James isn't righting the ship and demanding more from Belle. "Pay attention, Belle!" Mom interjects, interrupting the lesson. Now Belle knows something is wrong and feels badly that she isn't pleasing her mom. Worse still, the interruption has opened another topic for VIOLET Belle to process when she could be processing the technical point. Now her attention is divided between James's instruction and feeling guilty that she has failed Mom and wondering what she did wrong and what she can do to fix it. This is a huge and avoidable distraction. To avoid heaping blame (real or imagined) on VIOLET children, parents should avoid any interruption that will likely make the VIOLET child blame herself and feel like a failure. VIOLET is highly sensitive!

Acknowledging feelings will go a long way toward motivating VIOLET children because they are acutely aware of the emotional climate at all times. Taking a moment to acknowledge how the VIOLET child feels will help her productivity, not take her farther off track. It is the *most important* element.

Chapter 5: DESPITE *Life Lens*—ENVIRONMENT, PROCRASTINATION, and PRAISE

As long as you are primed for advice on how to communicate better with your children, I thought I would just mention a bit about the foundation that I have tried to bring to my teaching, even before I started using *Life Lens*, that is, creating an emotionally no-risk, no-fear learning environment.

Suzuki philosophy advocates changing the environment to effect change in the child. Shinichi Suzuki famously asserted, "Man is the son of his environment," (Hermann 1981) meaning that if you want to change the child, first you must change the environment. In other words, if your child doesn't want to work or do an activity with you, ask yourself, "How can I make the work environment more enticing to him?"

Regardless of a child or student's *Life Lens*, parents and teachers must establish a no-risk work environment where the child feels emotionally safe. This means eliminating sarcasm, lectures on how much lessons cost, threats, and yelling to try and get the student to sit down and focus. None of these approaches work, and all of them feel like anger to the child. Young children have no defense against parental anger. They want to please you, the parent. When they perceive your anger, it feels scary to them. Parents and teachers are the most important people in their life. When they sense anger around an activity or practice, it will seem to them as if the cause of the disruption in their all-important emotional relationship with you is the work itself! To avoid feeling your displeasure, they will avoid their work, which in turn only fuels your frustration, resulting in an unhappy cycle of negativity.

To create a no-risk environment, parents can focus on simply enjoying the time they spend with the child versus making the goal to "accomplish something." Establishing a friendly and pleasant routine together far outweighs the value of an unhappy practice time where you "got something done." Dr. Suzuki said, "An unhappy practice time is worse than no practice time."

Procrastination is not a *Life Lens*-specific phenomenon, whether we're talking about adults or children. For kids, sometimes just getting them to physically settle into the work or practice area is half the battle. One strategy Suzuki guitar co-founder Bill Kossler developed is called the "Oh Goody" Game. When Mom or Dad says, "It's time to practice/do homework," the student gets to put a sticker or point on a chart, or a marble in a jar if they respond, "Oh goody!" and run to their designated practice place to get out their instrument or work. When students have amassed a certain number of stickers, marbles, or points, they get to pick a fun activity to do with Mom or Dad. Not surprisingly, the "Oh Goody" Game works well with some kids and not so well with others.

Procrastination at its core relates to fear: fear of failure, fear of criticism, or fear of rejection if the task can't be accomplished. When a student puts off doing her work, it's her way of telling you that she feels insecure about something—usually how you, the parent, will respond to her. Procrastination often goes hand in hand with perfectionism. When people want to get something right, fear that they won't be able to get it right, and therefore delay starting the task to preserve the mentality that they *could* do it (when in reality they aren't doing anything), this seems preferable to actually trying to do the task and failing.

Psychologist Carol Dweck's book *Mindset* is a must-read if your child refuses to try and practice a new skill and then says things like, "Oh, this is SO easy for me," or "This is really boring." Such statements indicate what Dweck refers to as a *fixed mindset*—a crippling mental attitude that results when parents praise their child for things that the child does not control (Dweck 2008, 71–74). Statements such as, "You're so smart," or "You're amazing!" or "You're our little genius," actually serve to *discourage* the child from trying new things. Suppose they fail and expose that they're really NOT "so smart" or "a little genius"? A *fixed mindset* also reveals itself in perfectionism, where a student won't try something unless he is sure he can do it. Such a student may become frustrated or disconsolate when he makes a mistake. These kids care more about protecting their image of "being smart" than they do about learning from their mistakes. They correlate making mistakes with being a failure.

Parents can work with their children to help them develop a healthy *growth mindset* by praising them for their *hard work*. Instead of the above examples of praise, say things such as, "Wow, all that hard work you did really paid off," or "I like how you didn't give up, even when it got challenging," or "You did a great job figuring out how to solve that problem" (Dweck 2008, 177–178). The amount of effort a child puts into his work is something the child can always control. Parents and teachers can cultivate a *growth mindset* in their children by asking questions like:

"What did you learn today?"

"What mistake did you make today that taught you something?"

"What did you try hard at today?

Students with a *growth mindset* do not view failure as a devastating setback but rather as another opportunity to learn. People with a *growth mindset* can learn in *any* situation and often learn more from their failures than they do from their successes (Dweck 2008, 16–17).

Chapter 6: *Life Lens* DIAGNOSTIC TOOLS

By now you may have a good idea of what type of children you are working with. If not, the best way to figure it out is by observing their behavior and comparing what you see to the bullet points listed for each color section in chapter two. If you don't get a chance to observe your students enough or can't decide between two *Life Lens* types, this chapter should help you.

That said . . . **YOU DON'T NEED DIAGNOSTIC TOOLS!** Observable behavior is the best approach to determining *Life Lens* type. Apart from direct observation, the best diagnostics are the three tools I explain below: the Puzzle in the Baggie, the Picture of the Little Girl, and the Pirate's Treasure card game. If a discrepancy appears when using a diagnostic tool, *return to observable behavior* to make your determination of *Life Lens*. *Life Lens* can be clearly seen! Keep observing!

Many of my colleagues and studio parents have asked me for a diagnostic questionnaire, and, reluctantly, I have given in to their request. So, against my better judgment, you will find a flow chart at the end of this chapter with fourteen questions. The flow chart and questionnaire are my *least* favorite and least reliable tools, though. Please use them only as a *last resort* and not as the go-to diagnostic tool. Let me say it again: **YOU DON'T NEED DIAGNOSTIC TOOLS!** If you become adept at noticing the behavior of those around you, no extra diagnostics are necessary. Simply recognize and respect the behavior of the people with whom you interact. It's actually much faster and more organic than any external tool.

On an occasion when I'm asked to diagnose the *Life Lens* of a person I don't know, I first ask for a description of the person's behavior. This usually gives me all the information I need. If I'm wavering between two *Life Lens* types, my next step is to use one of my diagnostic activities.

REVERSE DIAGNOSTICS

Sometimes it's easier to first determine the person's learning style and then work back to figure out their *Life Lens*. For example, my former mother-in-law is a chatty, fun-loving person with a neatly organized home. Due to her sociability, I had always thought of her as GREEN. When I shared my ideas on the different types of visual learners with her, she exclaimed, "I learn the best when I can watch someone else do it first," and at that moment I realized that she is not GREEN but rather VIOLET—a watch-and-copy learner!

When I'm working with a student, I can confirm or deny my suspicions of their *Life Lens* by teaching them according to a particular learning style and observing how they respond. For instance, I had a boy in my guitar group class who was not my student. I only saw him for forty-five minutes once a week in a group with eight other kids. I had observed this boy talking to himself while playing alone during his brother's group class and thought that he might be an auditory learner (ORANGE). To test out my theory, I decided to conduct an experiment by having him say the technique he was working on out loud as we played together. It didn't help him; therefore, I knew that this boy was NOT an auditory learner and could not be ORANGE. I noticed that this student was extremely talkative but not the first one to talk to strangers, so I asked myself, "Which *Life Lens* talks to themselves when playing alone but isn't the first one to speak in a group of strangers?" The *Life Lens* types that fit that description are ORANGE or VIOLET. If the boy didn't respond well to saying and playing as an ORANGE auditory learner would, that meant he had to be VIOLET. To test my theory, I had the student watch one of his peers in the group and then copy him. The boy had success! VIOLET learns best by watching and copying. *Life Lens* confirmed.

If you have a verbally expressive student, but you're not certain whether or not she could be categorized as a "first talker" then you should try first ruling out RED or GREEN. Try to teach the student using a tactile element in the lesson. If the student doesn't respond well to the kinesthetic approach, that means she is not RED or GREEN. Change tactics and try teaching her the same thing in a visual written linear way—write it down in a step-by-step manner and show it to her. If she responds well, then you know she is INDIGO. (See an example of this below.)

In this photo, you see RED Jason working in a kinesthetic manner by rehearsing his right-hand guitar fingerings on his left cheek as he speaks them out loud to help him avoid repeating the same finger.

The picture above teaches the exact same principle of alternating right-hand fingers in a visual written linear way that INDIGO will best respond to. Artwork by Abigail Knight

If your student still doesn't seem to get it, change gears again and demonstrate what you want her to learn by having her watch you and then ask her to try it. If she can do it easily, then she is VIOLET, a visual watch-and-copy learner. (BLUE is also a watch-and-copy learner, but isn't a verbal expressive. If the student constantly asks questions and watches you like a hawk, she is likely BLUE.)

In the case of auditory learners, reverse diagnostics might not work as effectively. I have noticed that ORANGE students sometimes resist doing the one thing that will help them learn the best, namely, saying the material to be learned out loud. Therefore, it might be difficult to identify their learning style right away, even though ORANGE kids talk to themselves while playing alone (so do RED, GREEN, and VIOLET). One of the big clues that a person is ORANGE is if they get overwhelmed when you give them more than one thing to do at a time and if they are excellent at following directions. RED, GREEN, and VIOLET can handle many things thrown at them at once.

Some colors are similar in ways that can make them difficult to distinguish. Here are some examples:

RED vs. GREEN

First talkers are either RED or GREEN.

Both colors are visionary, competitive, stubborn, creative, like a challenge, rise to the occasion, catch on to things quickly. But…

RED

Does not get along well with everyone.

Does not care about pleasing people.

Doesn't mind standing alone.

Can keep a secret.

Values being right over relationships.

GREEN

Gets along well with everyone.

People pleasers.

Likes to have people around.

Can't keep a secret easily.

Values relationships over being right.

Which of these two people would you like to spend time with?

GREEN would rather spend time with #173.
RED would rather spend time with #357.

INDIGO vs. VIOLET

Both do quite a lot of talking, and they both read every spare moment for fun. But . . .

INDIGO
Pretty fast paced.
Time urgent; enjoys being under time pressure.

VIOLET
Much slower pace.
Time patient; can't stand time pressure.

BLUE vs. INDIGO

Both have a high standard of personal excellence, are linear thinkers, and are visual learners. Both like lists and learn things quickly. But . . .

BLUE
Does not like imposed artificial deadlines.

INDIGO
Loves deadlines and time pressure.

ORANGE vs. YELLOW

Both are time patient, slower paced, linear thinkers. But . . .

ORANGE
Likes to do one thing at a time and gets overwhelmed when asked to do multiple things simultaneously.

YELLOW
Wants to know all the elements of a given project up front.

Now, on to the diagnostic puzzles, which can be helpful when you are in a pinch and need a tool other than observable behavior to determine a person's *Life Lens.*

DIAGNOSTIC #1—Puzzle in a Baggie: "Can you complete this puzzle in thirty seconds?"

The baggie contains some random items I had lying around my house and provides no instructions. It's not readily apparent how or if the pieces fit together. I keep this small baggie with me and use it when strangers ask me what color they are. If you aren't keen on carrying your own baggie of odds and ends around, I've discovered that this diagnostic works just as well if you show a person the picture of the puzzle in a baggie and ask them: "Do you think you could complete this puzzle in thirty seconds or less?"

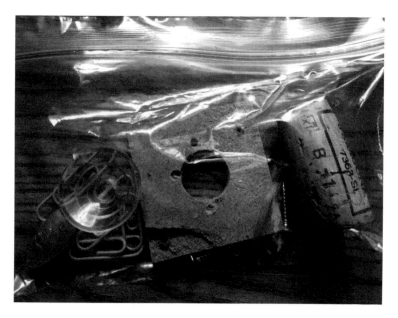

I created this diagnostic to differentiate between BLUE and INDIGO. Although I've gotten much quicker at identifying BLUE and INDIGO by observing their behavior, at first I sometimes had difficulty distinguishing between the two. Neither BLUE nor INDIGO talks first in a group of strangers, both are visual learners, and both are sensitive to time. Before I understood the nuances of how their visual learning styles and relationships to time differed, I needed a quick and organic assessment strategy. The Puzzle in a Baggie fit the bill! The key is whether or not the person is *willing to try* to complete the puzzle in thirty seconds or less. They don't have to actually do it.

When I show the baggie to a student and say, "Can you complete this puzzle in thirty seconds?" INDIGO will rise to the challenge and answer affirmatively: "Yes!" or "Sure," and will try to put the pieces together in thirty seconds. They might not succeed, but they will go for it.

When posed with the same question, BLUE answers with a *question* or a statement of confusion: "Wait, how is that a puzzle?" or "What's the point?" or "I don't even understand what that is, it looks like trash," and the person will *not* want to attempt it. The fact that there are no instructions on how to assemble the puzzle bothers BLUE. The fact that there is no example to follow makes attempting assembly under pressure a little too risky. Interestingly, once BLUE watches someone else attempt the puzzle, he will then be willing to try it also. No surprise there, since BLUE is a visual watch-and-copy learner.

The puzzle diagnostic reveals how a person responds to time pressure. INDIGO, who enjoys being under time pressure, will want to try to beat the clock to put the puzzle together. INDIGO only needs an objective—in this case, to assemble the contents of the bag—and she can figure out how to accomplish that objective. She doesn't need directions! INDIGO also thrives on a deadline—giving her thirty seconds engages her competitive nature.

BLUE, on the other hand, prefers to work according to his own internal sense of timing and does not enjoy being put under pressure in a new situation without any examples or instructions. BLUE is low risk. He doesn't want to look incompetent in front of others. BLUE would prefer to take the Puzzle in a Baggie home with him to practice outside of the public eye and then come back next week to show you how he can solve it in the allotted time.

Although the Puzzle in a Baggie was created to distinguish BLUE from INDIGO, it can be useful as a tool to determine other *Life Lens* types. RED and GREEN, both fast-paced and high risk-takers, will immediately take the challenge. Of course they can solve the puzzle in thirty seconds or less! Not knowing what the rules are doesn't stop competitive RED. She learns by doing so there's no reason not to jump in and tackle the Puzzle in a Baggie. If a RED fails, she'll just learn how *not* to do it next time.

GREEN is also a competitive, kinesthetic learner who will take the challenge just for fun. GREEN wants to please people and make friends, so he will happily take on the Puzzle in the Baggie challenge, because then he'll have something to talk to you about. Spatially oriented GREEN also enjoys working in three dimensions, so why not?

The other colors have much slower response times, so even though they might like to put the puzzle together, they will utterly disregard the thirty-second deadline. ORANGE, YELLOW, and VIOLET are time patient, meaning that they care more about doing high quality work than they do about meeting a deadline. It will take VIOLET more than thirty seconds just to look over the contents of the bag!

DIAGNOSTIC #2—Picture of the Little Girl: "What's going on in this picture?"

The Picture of the Little Girl has proven to be a fascinating way to quickly distinguish between ORANGE and YELLOW *Life Lens* types. Simply show the picture to your students and ask them, "What's going on in this picture?"

The ORANGE person responds: "I don't know." She might say something else before she says "I don't know," but eventually she will say, "I don't know." ORANGE does not have her own agenda. She won't try to make up a story about the picture. Interestingly, the ORANGE response of "I don't know" has held up whether the person was a four-year-old or a college professor!

YELLOW responds with a detailed description of the picture, such as: "The girl has a blue face and a white arm," or "The mouse has fallen off the desk," or "The girl is wearing a yellow skirt with eighteen purple polka dots." YELLOW notices small details that others may miss. YELLOW is non-judgmental and will stick to the facts of what he sees in the picture. One of my YELLOW colleagues referred to the creature on the stool as "some sort of animal" because he didn't want to commit to identifying it as a cat and have it turn out to be wrong. YELLOW cares deeply about accuracy and will give the most detailed description of the picture without offering any speculation—just the facts.

I originally turned to the Picture of the Little Girl diagnostic as a quick way to distinguish between ORANGE and YELLOW, and that's still my favorite way to use this visual. However, it's also interesting to note how other *Life Lens* types respond to the picture. I have noticed some common threads.

BLUE tends to give a short summary, describing things in the picture within some plausible conjecture on the context. BLUE does not speculate on the thoughts or feelings of the girl but will say things such as:

- "The girl is doing homework with her cat perched nearby, perhaps about to play with the mouse that is hanging off the desk," or
- "There's a girl at a desk, thinking or reading something. A cat is on a stool; there's a computer and pencil cup there also. The girl has pigtails and a spotted skirt—it's just a little scene of a girl at a desk," or
- "The mouse has fallen off the desk. The girl is sitting at the desk looking at a book or her computer."

INDIGO, a visual written linear learner and linear thinker, notices all the components of the picture in a step-by- step manner and then puts those components into a story, which might include something or someone outside of the picture! Here's an example:

"A girl is sitting at her desk, holding up a book as if she was reading it. You can also see some pens or pencils and a computer on the desk as well. On the right you can see a cat sitting on a chair that is almost as tall as the desk. Because of the way the girl is smiling and looking directly into the "camera" instead of concentrating on her book, the picture seems staged to me. The way the cat is sitting so that she is facing the camera instead of just lounging on the chair makes me think this shot was planned. The desk is completely organized except for the mouse hanging off the side. So really my answer to your question would be: Someone is taking a picture of a girl."

Here INDIGO concludes that the action is taking place by someone completely outside of the picture.

Another INDIGO said: "The little girl is thinking about something—I'm not sure what—and her cat looks at the girl and wants to know what she's looking at so she looks, too."

Again the focus is on looking at something that is happening *outside* of the actual picture and the protagonist is the cat. INDIGO is the only *Life Lens* type to give a personality to the cat!

A third INDIGO weighed in:

"I see a girl reading a book at her desk while her cat is trying to steal the computer. Well, that's kinda what I see because the cat has his/her tail out like a hook in the direction of the computer and the computer mouse is off the table so I thought that the cat had maybe knocked it off. And the girl doesn't notice because she is very interested in her book so she's not looking at that mischievous cat of hers.

"P.S. A little side note about the girl, why is one of the girl's arms white while the rest of her skin is blue?

"Why is the girl's head bigger than the computer screen?

"Why is the cat's head tan and the body white?"

In this example, the INDIGO creates a narrative about the *intent* of the mischievous cat to steal the computer and saves her detailed observations for the postscripts.

When looking at the picture of the little girl INDIGO often mentions the component of *reading*, perhaps because reading is so fundamental as the ultimate form of visual written linear learning.

VIOLET thinks in a circular manner, considering the components and then circling back to think about them in different ways. For this reason, it takes VIOLET the longest of any of the *Life Lens* types to respond to this seemingly simple question. The slow response time is a strong indication of VIOLET. When they eventually respond, VIOLET also goes outside the confines of the picture details, instead focusing on the girl and her internal landscape— what she is doing, thinking, or feeling. Some examples:

- "The girl is sitting at her desk reading, and the cat with the weird tail is hanging out with her, and someone knocked the mouse off the table."
- "I think she's posing for a picture. She doesn't look like she's thinking."
- "It's a little girl playing teacher with her cat."

VIOLET may also hone in on the *emotional* climate of the picture, saying:

- "It looks like a little girl in a happy mood at the computer."

- "This is a happy, confident girl, who is proudly showing the homework she has done—a very relaxed atmosphere."
- "A blue girl is reading to her cat. Her color is quite sickly, like she shouldn't be smiling so happily."

Both INDIGO and VIOLET read every spare moment for fun. They both love to engage in imaginary play—perhaps this explains why they go *outside* the picture in the case of INDIGO and *inside* what might be going on with the protagonist in the case of VIOLET.

RED and GREEN, both kinesthetic learners, will answer quickly with a creative story that ventures far away from the facts of the picture. Something like: "The girl has just received a letter from her best friend who recently moved to England. She's thinking about the last time she saw her friend and remembering all the fun they had together."

DIAGNOSTIC #3—Pirate Treasure Card Game

This is a good diagnostic for deciding between GREEN and VIOLET. If you don't want to make your own pirate cards, they are available at www.lifelensincolor.com

INSTRUCTIONS

- Print the cards out on heavy photo paper or card stock. There are four beautiful flowers, four pirate-themed items, four pirate teddy bears, and one golden treasure.
- Carefully cut out the cards.
- Spread the cards face down on a table.
- For every correct work task, the student gets to turn over a card. Repeat the process.

- The object is to find the treasure.
- How the student handles the cards is the key:

RED—enjoys the challenge of trying to find the treasure and will stop after they have found it.

GREEN—does not like this game at all. It violates her sense of cause and effect, that if she performs a task well, she should get a good reward. With Pirate Treasure, they only have a one in thirteen chance of finding the treasure. When I played this game with a three-year-old GREEN, the student lost interest and eventually walked away. If you play this game with a person who doesn't like it at all, she is GREEN.

ORANGE—loves this game and likes to put the cards into individual categories. He will put the beautiful flowers in one pile, the pirate items in another pile, and the teddy bears in a third pile.

YELLOW—likes this game. She turns the cards over and leaves them in place where they were. Once she finds the treasure, YELLOW still wants to turn over the rest of the cards to get the big picture. Once she has turned over all the cards, she might put them into categories.

BLUE—likes this game. When she turns a card over, she likes to carefully examine the picture. After BLUE has found the treasure, if you say, "We can play again, but you have to find the treasure in only two moves," she won't want to play again. Although BLUE likes the game initially, the appeal wears off once the student knows what all the cards look like.

INDIGO—also likes this game. The difference is after INDIGO has found the treasure, if you say, "We can play again, but you have to find the treasure in only two moves," INDIGO will want to try the new challenge.

VIOLET—loves this game. When he turns over a card, he may become carried away with it and lose track of trying to find the treasure. For instance, if VIOLET gets the Pirate Parrot, he may go into a monologue: "Squa-a-awck! I'm Pirate Parrot, flying around the ship. Flying is easier and faster than walking because I only have one leg. I can visit all my friends!" (Picture the VIOLET child flying the card around the room.) If VIOLET gets several Teddy Bears, he might say, "These guys are a team. They're going to help each other. This guy's name is Bob, this guy's name is Ralph, and this guy's name is Enrique." Because VIOLET has such a fantastic imagination he enjoys playing the PIRATE TREASURE game over and over, creating a new scenario every time.

And now, last and definitely least, the **FLOW CHART**…

Do you *like* flow charts?
YES! I like them a lot!
GREEN
YELLOW
VIOLET

NO! In fact, I *don't like* flow charts at all!
RED
ORANGE
BLUE
INDIGO

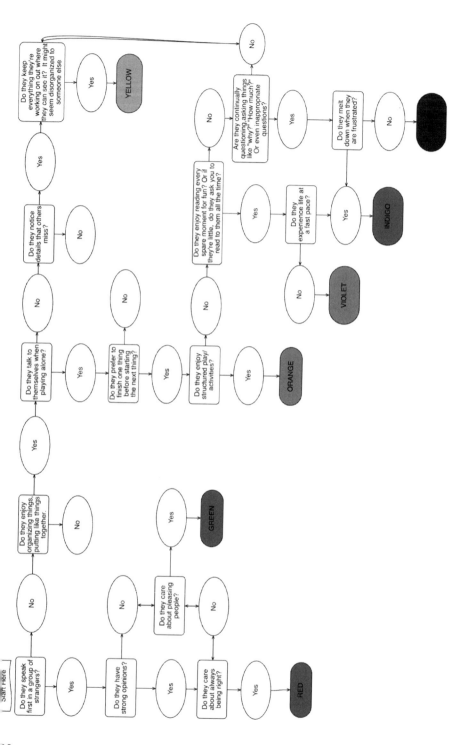

Start here

Do they speak first in a group of strangers?

Do they have strong opinions?

Do they care about always being right?

RED

Do they care about pleasing people?

GREEN

Do they enjoy organizing things, putting like things together?

Do they talk to themselves when playing alone?

Do they prefer to finish one thing before starting the next thing?

Do they enjoy structured play/activities?

ORANGE

Do they notice details that others miss?

Do they keep everything they're working on out where they can see it? It might seem disorganized to someone else

YELLOW

Do they enjoy reading every spare moment for fun? Or if they're little, do they ask you to read to them all the time?

Are they continually questioning, asking things like "why?" "How much?" Or even inappropriate questions?

Do they melt down when they are frustrated?

Do they experience life at a fast pace?

INDIGO

VIOLET

Life Lens Diagnostic Questions

Here's a linear presentation of the exact same information presented in the flow chart.

1. **Do they talk first in a group of strangers?**
2. **Do they care about pleasing people?**
3. **Do they have strong opinions?**
4. **Do they care about always being right?**
5. **Do they enjoy categorizing things, putting like things together?**
6. **Do they talk to themselves when playing alone?**
7. **Do they prefer to finish one thing before starting the next thing?**
8. **Do they enjoy structure? (structured play/activities)**
9. **Do they read every spare moment just for fun? If it's a young child, do they want you to read to them all the time?**
10. **Do they experience life at a fast pace?**
11. **Are they continually asking questions, such as "why?" or "how much?" or even inappropriate questions?**
12. **Do they melt down when they are frustrated?**
13. **Do they notice small details that others miss?**
14. **Do they keep everything they're working on out where they can see it, even if it looks disorganized to you?**

KEY:

1. **Do they talk first in a group of strangers?** RED and GREEN will often talk first in a group of strangers. They are verbally expressive and appear very animated when they're with others. INDIGO and VIOLET are also

quite talkative but not usually the first ones to speak in a group of strangers. INDIGO and VIOLET are verbally expressive when others initiate conversation.

2. **Do they care about pleasing people?** ORANGE, GREEN, BLUE, and VIOLET care about pleasing people. In the stream of the flow chart, if you have a person who talks first in a group of strangers and cares about pleasing people, he is GREEN.

3. **Do they have strong opinions?** RED people have strong opinions about everything. They are the most opinionated *Life Lens*. GREEN people may have strong opinions, but they might not always share their opinions, whereas RED always expresses her view.

4. **Do they care about always being right?** RED cares more about being right than about maintaining relationships. GREEN cares more about maintaining relationships than about being right. YELLOW cares about accuracy and precision but are the least judgmental, whereas RED is the most judgmental.

5. **Do they enjoy categorizing things, putting like things together?** ORANGE, YELLOW, BLUE, INDIGO and VIOLET all enjoy categorizing things.

6. **Do they talk to themselves when playing alone?** ORANGE and VIOLET talk to themselves when playing or working alone, and, to a lesser extent, RED and GREEN may also talk to themselves.

7. **Do they prefer to finish one thing before starting the next thing?** ORANGE, BLUE, and INDIGO prefer to finish one thing before starting the next, but only ORANGE is a true "monotasker."

8. **Do they enjoy structure?** ORANGE really loves structure. BLUE also likes structure. INDIGO and VIOLET prefer unstructured play based on imagination.

9. **Do they read every spare moment for fun?** INDIGO and VIOLET always have a book in their hands.

10. **Do they experience life at a fast pace?** INDIGO experiences life at a fast pace, but VIOLET experiences life at the slowest pace of all. (RED, GREEN and BLUE also experience life at a fast pace.)

11. **Are they continually questioning, asking "why?" or "how much?" or even inappropriate questions?** BLUE constantly questions everything. RED often wants to know "why," but the hallmark of BLUE is their curiosity and constant inquiry.

12. **Do they melt down when they are frustrated?** INDIGO kids melt down when they are frustrated. BLUE will not. Outside this stream of the flow chart ORANGE and VIOLET can melt down, but RED, YELLOW, and GREEN usually do not.

13. **Do they notice small details that others miss?** YELLOW and VIOLET do notice small details that others miss. To distinguish between them, test for Visual Written Diagrammatic or Visual Watch-and-Copy learning styles. ORANGE may also notice small details. Test for auditory learning style.

14. **Do they keep everything they're working on out where they can see it, even if it appears disorganized to someone else?** YELLOW wants everything they're currently working on visible so that they don't forget anything. Having everything they need out where they

need it constitutes functional space to YELLOW, even though it might appear chaotic to an onlooker. VIOLET cares about having a beautiful aesthetic space where everything is in its place and is functioning perfectly. Disorganized space bothers VIOLET.

APPENDIX: THE IKEA TOOL

At some point, everyone has purchased furniture that required assembly. Just for fun, here's how each *Life Lens* handles IKEA furniture.

RED hates to go to IKEA because you can't just run in, buy what you want, and leave. The layout of the store is such that you are trapped in a maze of all things Swedish. AAAAAAARGHH! The meatballs are pretty good, but, overall, shopping at IKEA is hell for RED people. Therefore, they are more likely to order the item online and have it delivered to avoid the IKEA experience. Once they get the furniture, RED people enjoy putting it together, but they might not look at the directions. They have to learn by doing, so it's like a big puzzle. Once they have it put together, RED people will then physically move the furniture around to see how it looks in different places in the room. They have to learn by DOING, so no drawing will substitute for actually seeing the thing in this spot and then in that spot.

ORANGE people like IKEA when they know what they are looking for, or at least the general type of thing they need (sofa, chairs, lighting). Just wandering around aimlessly in IKEA will frustrate ORANGE. They can avoid the potentially overwhelming experience by ordering online.

YELLOW people will first make a detailed diagram of their room dimensions and figure out exactly where the proposed furniture will fit the best. Functionality reigns supreme for YELLOW. If the item also looks nice it's a plus but not necessary if it serves its purpose. A YELLOW person might draw and re-draw the layout many times before he is ready to actually purchase the furniture, and YELLOW tends to be cheap, so he will look for a sale or some kind of deal before he actually buys the item. YELLOW people are patient. You can't hurry them into a quick decision. When they eventually get the furniture, they have already figured out down to the inch where it will go. They assemble the furniture to bring into reality what they had already thought out and sketched.

GREEN thinks IKEA is fun! They enjoy the whole concept of IKEA and the ease of shopping there. Having a giant variety of items, including a restaurant, appeals to GREEN. They like that there is something for everyone, including convenient babysitting for the kids.

BLUE has a wonderful sense of style and intuitively knows what will look good. They may consult magazines to see what's "in" and to get ideas for their room. BLUE people also like to shop, so they enjoy going to IKEA and spending hours looking at all the various items and displays that are all conveniently organized. When they make the purchase, they somehow always get a good deal! They then find someone else to assemble the furniture for them.

INDIGO likes IKEA. The über organization of the place appeals to them. In fact, the founder of IKEA, Ingvar Kamprad, is INDIGO! Frugality and enthusiasm aptly describe INDIGO people. They excel at taking the meager resources around them and using them to create something awesome. As a child, Ingvar Kamprad bought matches in bulk and then sold them individually at a low price and still made a good profit. After matches he expanded to selling flower seeds, greeting cards, Christmas tree decorations, and later pencils and ballpoint pens. Ingvar Kamprad flies economy class and writes on both sides of the paper even though he is one of the wealthiest men in the world. INDIGO also likes to follow rules. Ingvar Kamprad actually states, "I am very proud to follow the rules of our company."

INDIGO people excel at creating systems or frameworks for people to accomplish things. Here is the IKEA concept from their website www.ikea.com:

Anybody can make a good-quality product for a high price, or a poor-quality product for a low price. But to make good products at low prices, you need to develop methods that are both cost-effective and innovative. This has been the focus of IKEA since its beginnings in Småland, Sweden. Maximising the use of raw materials and production adaptation to meet people's needs and preferences has meant that our costs are low. The IKEA way of doing things is to pass these cost savings on to you, our customers.

INDIGO is always *busy*, making things bigger, better, faster, farther. Ingvar Kamprad sums it up when he says: "I'm not afraid of turning 80, and I have lots of things to do. I don't have time for dying."

VIOLET has to think a long time about the furniture and will read and research online to their satisfaction before venturing into IKEA. When they get there, they love to look around and imagine how each item would look in their house. This distracts them from their original task, but eventually they will circle back around to the furniture they came to buy. They might also make sketches of their space. It will take them forever to make a decision, and once they finally pull the trigger on the purchase and get the furniture home they can't put it together right away. No. They have to imagine how they would feel if the furniture was over in the corner. How would it affect the flow of the room? How would it look? How would they feel if the furniture was on the other wall? They have to sit with the unopened box in the room and just imagine all the possible permutations. It might be days or even weeks before they attempt to open the box and put together the furniture. When they finally get around to assembling it, it will be done meticulously and will enhance the room in both functionality and beauty. It will be perfect.

Life Lens PRACTICE DO'S and DON'TS

RED DO'S

- Do play competitive games
- Do allow them to use their creativity to solve problems
- Do use metaphors and analogies
- Do challenge them
- Do provide strong, decisive leadership
- Do incorporate a tactile component
- Do rehearse left-hand fingerings on the right arm and right-hand fingerings on the left cheek
- Do let them teach you the skill they are trying to learn
- Do use a non-judgmental prop to deliver suggestions
- Do have them sing/speak/hum while playing
- Do give them incremental deadlines

RED DON'TS

- Don't play open-ended games
- Don't use charts—not fun!
- Don't be wishy washy
- Don't use stickers
- Don't be hard on them when they make a mistake
- Don't always use the same practice routine

ORANGE DO'S

- Do verbally affirm them
- Do have them SAY OUT LOUD whatever they're learning
- Do let them ACCUMULATE things when they perform a successful repetition
- Do give them a clear objective
- Do give them plenty of time to do the job right
- Do point out how what they're doing is helpful to others (you, the teacher, classmates)
- Do establish a consistent routine

ORANGE DON'TS

- Don't give them lots of choices (open-endedness is too unclear and stressful)
- Don't use analogies and metaphors
- Don't give them linear charts
- Don't give them more than one thing on which to focus
- Don't put them under time pressure
- Don't use recognition as a motivator (they don't like to draw attention to themselves)

YELLOW DO'S

- Do use diagrams, charts, and pictures
- Do use stickers
- Do show them all of the components necessary to do the activity up front
- Do give them plenty of time
- Do use factoids. After every successful repetition give them a random fact
- Do show instead of tell
- Do use lists
- Do make sure their practice space is functional (everything they need is where they can see it)

YELLOW DON'TS

- Don't put them on the spot
- Don't talk too much
- Don't unexpectedly change the plan
- Don't be hard on them when they make a mistake
- Don't throw a lot of things at them all at once
- Don't give them a lot of choices

GREEN DO'S

- Do encourage them to do high-quality work to achieve a high-quality result
- Do focus on cause and effect, "What happens when your finger does *this*? What happens when your finger does *that*?"
- Do let them know that you (the parent) are on their side
- Do leave all correcting/fixing to the teacher
- Do incorporate a tactile component/physical activity into what they're doing
- Do practice things they can already do, and work on making these things even better
- Do work in small increments, such as two measures at a time
- Do ask them, "What can you do to make the next one even better?"
- Do physically keep track of the number of correct repetitions (bead counter, pennies on a music stand)
- Do write down all necessary information in one place where they can see it
- Do rehearse left-hand fingerings on the right arm and right-hand fingerings on the left cheek
- Do have them sing/speak/hum while playing
- Do ask them for ideas on how to make the given activity more fun

GREEN DON'TS

- Do NOT attempt to correct or fix *anything* during home practice!
- Don't always give them the answer, instead encourage them to figure it out
- Don't cover large amounts of material all at once (they will likely miss important details)
- Don't allow them to employ more personality than actual hard work on the given task
- Don't forget to play games and to have fun!

BLUE DO'S

- Do SHOW them what to do
- Do break down skills into easily manageable parts
- Do video important concepts
- Do give them practice charts/checklists
- Do make sure they understand WHY they have to do it
- Do inspire them with expert performances (either in person or video)
- Do reward them periodically for their excellent work (the reward should be something that BLUE has selected)
- Do use cool looking stickers (bland stickers are not motivating!)
- Do take all time pressure off of them

BLUE DON'TS

- Don't put them on the spot
- Don't threaten them
- Don't push them beyond their own pace
- Don't play games during home practice (BLUE finds them annoying). Young BLUE students will enjoy practice games that look cool when they are beginners
- Don't talk too much
- Don't put them under time pressure

INDIGO DO'S

- Do challenge them
- Do play competitive games
- Do keep track of the quality of repetitions with cards or anything—good goes in this pile; bad goes in this pile
- Do ask them "Can you get more in the 'good' pile this time?"
- Do put them under time pressure
- Do find ways for them to go BIGGER, BETTER, FARTHER, and FASTER (principle of ESCALATION)
- Do give them a lot to do
- Do give them new information in a WRITTEN LINEAR manner
- Do use analogy and metaphor when teaching or correcting technique
- Do use charts and planners
- Do verbally praise their hard work

INDIGO DON'TS

- DON'T BORE THEM
- Don't give them a set number of repetitions
- Don't play open-ended games
- Don't make up rules as you go
- Don't break the rules
- Don't micromanage them
- Don't use diagrams
- Don't fail to recognize their accomplishments great or small

VIOLET DO'S

- Do engage their imagination *with limits* ("you can tell me one thing about this picture")
- Do incorporate instrumental practice (or the given activity) into a larger ecosystem that VIOLET creates as they go
- Do show them the toy, cards, thing you plan to use with them in the practice time up front
- Do tell them "every time you play one repetition, you will get one of these (the aforementioned toy, cards)
- Do play open-ended games
- Do DEMONSTRATE
- Do be patient with their slow pace
- Do inspire them with expert recordings, videos, and concerts
- Do use BINARY language (more or less, louder or softer, this or that)
- Do ACKNOWLEDGE their feelings (every time about everything)
- Do be emotionally supportive
- Do use language such as "I wonder what would happen if . . ." "I'm curious how trying *this* would make it sound?"
- Do tell them how much you liked their effort (even if the result was a total failure) and say, "I'm curious what it would sound like if you tried *this*?"
- Do keep them in a predictable routine
- Do give them as much advance notice as possible if their routine is going to change

- Do put them in the front row in a class setting to minimize distraction
- Do give them plenty of time to do the job

VIOLET DON'TS

- Don't use direct commands
- Don't challenge them (they give up easily)
- Don't tell them they did a bad job
- Don't put them under time pressure
- Don't abruptly change their routine
- Don't play competitive games
- Don't play complicated games (you will never get them back to the original activity)

REFERENCES

Arad, A., Feige, K. (Producers) and Favreau, J. (Director).
2008. *Iron man* [Motion picture]. United States: Paramount Pictures, Marvel Studios.

Bilan, A. 2012. *Lebron James made of Skittles* [Collage]. Retrieved from http://www.behance.net.

Becker, C. 2007. "Dress for success." *Seventeen*, November 19. Retrieved from http://www.seventeen.com/fashion/advice/a9119/vera-wang-sept06/

Booker T. Washington quotes. n.d. Retrieved from http://www.goodreads.com/author/quotes/84278.Booker_T_Washington.

Brennan, S. (Producer). 2009. *NCIS: Los Angeles* [Television series]. United States: CBS Television Studios.

Brennan, S. (Writer) and Whitmore, Jr., J. (Director). 2011. "Familia" [Television series episode]. In Brennan, S. (Producer). *NCIS: Los Angeles*. United States: CBS Television Studios. Retrieved from ncisla.wikia.com.

Burk, A. 2000. *The Redemptive Gifts of Individuals* [CD]. Anaheim, CA: Sapphire Leadership Group.

Burk, A. 2005. *The Sound of Light* [CD]. Grandview, MO: Plumbline Publishing.

Duff, J., Shephard, G., Belanoff, A., Wallace, R. (Producers). 2012. *Major Crimes* [Television series]. Los Angeles, CA: Warner Bros. Television.

Dweck, C. S. 2008. *Mindset: The New Psychology of Success*. New York, NY: Ballantine Books.

Faber, A., and Mazlish, E. 1980. *How to talk so kids will listen and listen so kids will talk*. New York, NY: Rawson, Wade Publishers.

FDCH E-media. 2004, November 18. *Former president Clinton speaks at library dedication* [Transcript]. Retrieved from http://www.washingtonpost.com/wp-dyn/articles/A60393-2004Nov18.html

Feige, K. (Producer) and Favreau, J. (Director). 2010. *Iron Man 2* [Motion picture]. United States: Paramount Pictures, Marvel Studios.

Fellowes, J., (Writer) and Bolt, B. (Director). 2010. Series, 1, Episode 3 [Television series episode]. In Trubridge, L. (Producer). *Downtown Abbey*. London, UK: Carnival Films.

Fitzpatrick, T. 2013, April 30. "Vera Wang Says Keep Your Feet on the Ground and Don't Get Ahead of Yourself." *The Business of Fashion*. Retrieved from http://www.businessoffashion.com/articles/first-person/first-person-vera-wang.

Garcia, R., 2013, December 19. *The most inspiring famous failures*. Retrieved from http://blog.megafounder.com/blog/most-famous-failures/.

Geter, L. (Writer) and Geter, L. (Director). 2012. "The Shame Game" [Television series episode]. In Duff, J., Shephard, G., Belanoff, A., Wallace, R. (Producers). *Major Crimes*. Los Angeles, CA: Warner Bros. Television.

Gevers, J.M.P., Mohammed, S. and Baytalskaya, N. 2014. "The Conceptualisation and Measurement of Pacing Styles." *Applied Psychology: An International Review*, accepted or in press.

Haftmann, W., translated by Baumann, H. and Brown, A. 1984. *Chagall*. New York, NY: Harry N. Abrams Inc.

Hanson, H. (Creator) and Reichs, K., Deschanel, E., Boreanaz, D. (Producers). 2005. *Bones* [Television series]. United States: Josephson Entertainment, Far Field Productions, 20th Century Fox Television.

Harriss, J.A. 2003, December. "The Elusive Marc Chagall." *Smithsonian Magazine*. Retrieved from http://www.smithsonianmag.com/arts-culture/the-elusive-marc-chagall-95114921/?no-ist.

Hermann, E. 1981. *Shinichi Suzuki: The Man and His Philosophy*. Miami, FL: Summy-Birchard Music, division of Summy-Birchard Inc.

Howard Schultz biography. n.d. Retrieved from http://www.biography.com/people/howardschultz-21166227.

Ingvar Kamprad quotes. n.d. Retrieved from http://www.inspirationalstories.com/quotes/im-not-afraid-of-turning-80-and-of-ingvar-kamprad-quote/.

Introvert and Extravert. 2014. In *Encyclopædia Britannica*. Retrieved from http://www.britannica.com/topic/introvert.

Madigan, J. B. 2009. *Building better brains through movement* [PDF document]. Retrieved from http://www.abllab.com.

Mohammed, S., and Harrison, D. 2013. The clocks that time us are not the same: A theory of temporal diversity, task characteristics, and performance in teams. *Organizational Behavior and Human Decision Processes*, 122(2), 244-256.

Noah Webster. n.d. Retrieved from http://webstersdictionary1828.com/NoahWebster.

Oprah Winfrey Quotes. n.d. Retrieved from http://www.goodreads.com/author/quotes/3518.Oprah_Winfrey?page=4.

Oprah Winfrey's Official Biography. 2011, May 17. Retrieved from http://www.oprah.com/pressroom/Oprah-Winfreys-Official-Biography#ixzz3qm8B-tOJJ.

Rachael Ray Quotes. n.d. Retrieved from http://www. evancarmichael.com/library/rachael-ray/Rachael-Ray-Quotes.html.

Scorsese, M. (Director). 2001. *Hugo* [Motion picture]. United States: Paramount. Retrieved from http://www. imdb.com.

Seigneur, E. 2013, August 15. "Ask a Neuroscientist: How to Train Your Brain." Retrieved from https://neuroscience.stanford.edu/news/ask-neuroscientist-how-train-your-brain.

Suzuki, S. 1983. *Nurtured by Love: The Classic Approach to Talent Education* (2nd Ed.) (W. Suzuki, Trans.). Miami, FL: Suzuki Method International.

The IKEA way. n.d. Retrieved from http://www.ikea.com/ ms/en_GB/about_ikea/the_ikea_way/.

The Ray Kroc Story. 2009. Retrieved from http://www.mcdonalds.com/us/en/our_story/our_history/the_ ray_kroc_story.html.

Titcher, D., Roskin, M., Peak, K. (Producers) and Winther, P. (Director). 2004. *The Librarian: Quest for the Spear*. [Made-for-television original movie]. United States: Turner Network Television.

Wloszczyna, S. 2013, August 15. "Jobs" [Review of the film *Jobs*]. Retrieved from http://www.rogerebert.com/ reviews/jobs-2013.

ACKNOWLEDGMENTS

"For as we have many members in one body,
but all the members do not have the same
function . . . These gifts show our capacity."
-Arthur Burk, *The Redemptive Gifts of Individuals*

When I first heard Arthur Burk's (2000) teaching on the redemptive gifts of individuals, I had my "Aha!" moment. I realized that the thing that made me associate one student or family with another was that they had the same redemptive gift, which meant that they had similar observable behavior. This is what fueled my quest to find ways to help me explain what made different students receptive to different kinds of teaching and learning, and what made their relationships with their parents succeed or fail when it came to learning music. Burk (2005) also lead me along the path toward organizing the ideas behind *Life Lens* into color categories. His "Sound of Light" lecture inspired me to search for other manifestations of "light," and my research eventually made me see my students, all of our children, as symbols of light themselves. Eureka! It became clear that there was no better way to identify the seven *Life Lens* types than by the seven visible colors of the electromagnetic spectrum, otherwise known as the colors of the rainbow: RED, ORANGE, YELLOW, GREEN, BLUE, INDIGO, and VIOLET.

I am indebted to Dr. Susan Mohammed (2013), whose research on how individuals relate to time and deadlines helped me explain why some children would play a game and never want to come back to the task at hand, and why time constraints energize some children but are a motivation killer for others. Mohammed's work helped me define the differences at work when parents were in a hurry with kids who weren't and how destructively powerful time orientation can be. She also gave me valuable feedback as a first reader!

If not for the invaluable work of these two teachers and researchers, *Life Lens* might never have come together as a cohesive system, and for that I am grateful!

There's one person who has been there, helping me sharpen my focus and challenging me along the many years of our shared Suzuki journey—my daughter, Mercedes. I'm sorry I didn't realize a lot sooner that we are not the same! Thank you for your patience with me while I was figuring it out and for your amazing, timely insights, many of which appear in this book. None of this would have been possible without you!

Amy Plattsmier, my editor, thank you doesn't even begin to cover it! Your thorough and creative touch made this book SO much better than it would have been otherwise. Thank you for pushing me over the finish line.

I am so grateful for the immeasurable contributions from so many of my former and current Suzuki students and their families, especially:

Angela Ortiz and the Khambhla family, the Knight family, the Moeck family, Nancy Lin and the Farmer family, the Orbegozo family, Amy Plattsmier and the Gonsky family, the Sullivan family, the Maloney family, the Parks family, the Wagner family, the Warner family, the Fern family, the Kelley family, the Khakoo family, the Perdue family, the Salib family, Cori SaNoGuiera and the Farstrup family, the Pallone family, the Frisoli family, Andrea Alban-Davies and the Albarracin family, the Perna family, the McHale family, the St. Pierre family, the Weber family, the

Crawmer family, Kristen Hallett and the Sclafani family, the Fulton family, the Meyer family, the Welch family, and *all* of my other studio families throughout the years.

Most of all, I appreciate how you have opened your lives and hearts to me and for the many wonderful hours that we have spent together around learning to play the guitar. I feel like I've learned more from you than you have from me! It's a joy and an honor to get to have you in my life. Without you, this book would not have been possible.

Thank you to my dear friends Mila Sahakian, Nancy Dinning, Marianne Kao, Megan Sweeney, Zeah Riordan, and Andrea Cannon for your steadfast encouragement.

Thank you to my first readers—Susan Mohammed, Katherine Anderson, Gary Marcus, Brian Thomas Moser, and Paisley Davidson—for your intelligent and honest feedback.

Huge thanks to Regan Dockery for stepping in at the last minute and creating the Marbles in a Tube and Little Girl illustrations.

Thanks to Ed Sprunger for your sage and timely advice.

Thanks to Rini Bunjaj Dream Waves Salon and Victoria, Carmen, and all my friends at Devachan.

Thank you to my Suzuki colleagues Julianne Carney, Madeleine Davidson, Stephanie Giorgio, James Wellington (creator of the amazing "Rules Tower" concept), Noelle Perrin, Laura Mazza-Dixon, and Christopher and Elissah Becknell for your insight and input and for testing out my ideas to see if they would actually work with your students!

Thanks to Nick and Heather Hardie, my colleagues at the Greenwich Suzuki Academy, and all of my friends at the Brooklyn Conservatory of Music—Fa Jihada, Jeri Choi, Liz Lewis-John,

Katie Denton, and Karen Geer—high fives all around! Thank you to Victoria Grager, Erin Paglia, Laura Victoir, Jane Brill, Juliette Spertus, Dinah Nissen, Dorothy Savitch, and Kristina Nebel for your observations and input.

Thanks, Mom and Dad!

In the words of Johann Sebastian Bach, I dedicate this book, "To the glory of God and the edification of my fellows."

Michele Monahan Horner
Cos Cob, Connecticut

ABOUT THE AUTHOR

Michele Horner has been a Suzuki guitar teacher since 2000. Known for her innovative ideas and dynamic presentation style, Michele has been featured as a clinician at Suzuki Institutes and Workshops all over the U.S. Her students were selected by audition to perform a featured concert at the 13th Suzuki World Convention in Torino, Italy in 2006. Michele was on the faculty of the first International Suzuki Guitar Festival in 2008 and the 14th Suzuki World Convention in Melbourne, Australia in 2009. Her lecture "Listening Like a Maniac" has been viewed over 10,000 times and is in the permanent video collection of the Suzuki Association of the Americas.

She is the creator of an Interactive Journey through Art & Music (IJAM), a workshop that makes connections between visual art, sculpture, architecture and music through historical epochs. In 2010 Michele was Artist In Residence at the Suzuki Charter School in Edmonton, Alberta, where she focused on applying principles from an Interactive Journey through Art & Music to academic subjects at the K-6 elementary school.

Michele is a graduate of Penn State University where she still holds school records in field hockey goalkeeping. She studied classical guitar with Kevin Gallagher and Fred Hand and is on the faculty of the Greenwich Suzuki Academy in Connecticut and is the Head of the Suzuki Guitar Department of the Brooklyn Conservatory of Music in New York.

www.lifelensincolor.com